A Good Day at School

A GOOD DAY at School

Take Charge of EMOTIONS so Your Child Can Find HAPPINESS

Kat Mulvaney

NEW YORK

LONDON • NASHVILLE • MELBOURNE • VANCOUVER

A Good Day at School

Take Charge of Emotions so Your Child Can Find Happiness

Published in New York, New York, by Morgan James Publishing in partnership with Difference Press. Morgan James is a trademark of Morgan James, LLC. www.MorganJamesPublishing.com

ISBN 9781642796506 paperback
ISBN 9781642796513 eBook
ISBN 9781642797190 audiobook

Library of Congress Control Number: 9781642797190

Cover Design by:
Chris Treccani
www.3dogcreative.net

Interior Design by:
Christopher Kirk
www.GFSstudio.com

Morgan James is a proud partner of Habitat for Humanity Peninsula and Greater Williamsburg. Partners in building since 2006.

Get involved today! Visit
MorganJamesPublishing.com/giving-back

To parents who felt an existential shift when their children were born, who yearn for more connection, and who want to break the generational cycle of unconsciousness. And to VR and TF, whose light reminded me of my own.

CONTENTS

ON CHILDREN

Your children are not your children.
They are the sons and daughters
of Life's longing for itself.
They come through you but not from you,
And though they are with you yet they belong not to you.

You may give them your love but not your thoughts,
For they have their own thoughts.
You may house their bodies but not their souls,
For their souls dwell in the house of tomorrow,
which you cannot visit, not even in your dreams.
You may strive to be like them,
but seek not to make them like you.
For life goes not backward nor tarries with yesterday.

You are the bows from which your children
as living arrows are sent forth.
The archer sees the mark upon the path of the infinite,
and He bends you with His might
that His arrows may go swift and far.
Let your bending in the archer's hand be for gladness;
For even as He loves the arrow that flies,
so He loves also the bow that is stable.

–Kahlil Gibran

Chapter 1:

THE CALL FROM SCHOOL

You did everything the doctor said to do while you were pregnant, you breastfed, and you love your child more than anything else. So when the teacher called on the second week of preschool to report your child had bitten another classmate, you were horrified and hoped it was a one-time thing. When he came to you trembling at a birthday party asking to go home, you could tell he was overwhelmed and wondered if your precious child had anxiety. When the school said he couldn't return after spring break due to tantrums, your heart broke under the weight of rejection for your child and yourself. The behavior he was accused of wasn't unfounded, but you could see how volatile he was and how consumed with emotions he had become. Why does he seem to struggle more than the other kids? Why is he so affected? You talked to your pediatrician, who first said to get him more exercise, but team sports led to meltdowns and awkward glares. Eventually you stop going. Next, the doctor recommended medication, and at first you resisted. The two you did try had frightening side effects and one made him lose weight. Neither helped his emotions. And your momma-gut said medication wasn't the answer. A therapist said to look for a smaller class size and a school that is more understanding of children with "special needs," but even with intervention from school, your child says he hates it and reports being teased.

You don't want to leave your child somewhere he hates, but you have to work and take care of your other children. You want your child to be happy and enjoy learning and friendships. You want to drop him off at school or an activity and not watch your phone, worried that an incident has occurred. You made excuses to keep him home from birthday parties and eventually the invitations stopped. At home, your child is calmer and enjoys learning and playing on his own. But is isolation healthy for a child? You've considered homeschooling him, but are you qualified for that, and what happens in middle school and high school? You cannot keep him by your side, managing the stress and worry forever. You also rely on being able to work and do some amount of self-care while your children are in school, and with him home every day your health and other relationships suffer. You love your family but cannot give this much on a mostly empty cup.

Not satisfied with the discipline-or-medicate advice you were given, you've scoured the internet and your town for less drastic approaches for your child. You tried the supplements, bought a book on kid's yoga, tried multiple therapists, and walked in and right back out of karate because it was too loud for your child. You adjusted diet, removing dairy and gluten, and have tried to reduce sugar and preservatives, and while diet does affect his behavior and mood, it's near impossible to control food when out of the house and around other children. You're curious about things like meditation and have heard terms like cranial sacral and Reiki, but the nearest practitioner is one hundred miles away one way. If the medical community has nothing to offer your child, surely there is an alternative you haven't found yet.

Once you explained to a teacher and administrator how smart your child is despite his hard-to-manage emotions. They agreed but said they were not equipped to meet his needs. You'd have to look into private schools and specialists, which were expensive, but you found the money. Why couldn't they help the kids develop their individual strengths, focus on getting them more exercise while at school, or teach them stress management? You wished they knew how big his heart was and how hard he cries after an emotional episode. He just feels differently than other children. He feels deeper. You can tell he sees the world differently too. You know there must be a solution or place for him, and you won't stop until he is happy, thriving, and back in a school he loves.

You are not alone. The American school system expects children to be identical, watching for a slight difference to label or diagnose, which tells children as young as five that they are not good enough or worthy of patience or compassion. If a child cannot sit on the carpet square for the duration of circle time, the child is deemed unruly. If a child does not learn or behave like the others, he's called special needs and treated differently, as if he isn't already isolated with his overwhelming feelings. Children are not allowed to be themselves, but that's all they can be. Asking children to change or suppress their truth is what is driving the out-of-control emotions, depression, and rampant suicide among children, teens, and young adults. And problems are extending beyond just individual children. In the United States, the number of school or public shootings carried out by tormented and hurting kids, looking for revenge or relief, is increasing at a horrifying pace. Thousands of children are struggling in ways older generations didn't experience and don't understand. These are symptoms of a broken system, several of them in fact, and there is slow improvement in some areas and hopelessness in others. Parents and adults who love kids and recognize these issues must step up and find new solutions, solutions as unique and bright as the children who need them. It's time for these broken systems to fail because they are not evolving to keep up with our children, and special souls are falling through the cracks. In the meantime, there are tools that will empower your whole family and bring you some greatly deserved peace.

Chapter 2:

THE LONG WAY

I believe we choose our parents before we are conceived, while we are acting from the highest version of ourselves and are still one with the creator of all things, our source–God. I chose my parents for the purpose of one day helping other parents help their children make sense of existential concepts like where we come from and why we're here and also to understand our evolving planet, but most importantly, I chose them to save kids' lives. My parents gave me the experience I now see would best bring light to the planet and keep other children–millions of them–from living the darkness I knew as a young person. My specialty would be emotions, which are really just little bits of energy we can feel in ways we don't understand. Many sensitive people can feel the emotions of others, the feelings of animals, or the energy around an object, for example; and growing up with this gift, yet having no information or support about it, can make life excruciating. Emotions make us uncomfortable and confused when they are not our own, and I teach families how to protect themselves from ones brought on by outside forces. But when emotions are all our own and pure, even when they feel hard, they bring us the joy of sledding down a snowy hill or the excitement of buying a first home, and they offer us the chance for growth in the form of frustration or admiration.

I learned how to help parents understand their child's emotions through contrast. I had to experience emotional duress myself and wanted to die for many years in order to relate to struggling kids and families. In the same way we can only truly appreciate the sunny beaches of Hawaii after living through a rainy American Pacific Northwest winter, I chose to be brought into a family where there was little happiness, joy, compassion, or connection to something greater than us. My parents did not know they were sentencing me to a life with little joy and happiness because they were not modeling or creating any around me. As a child, I was watching every move they made, and what I saw was struggle, depression, the weight of obligation, and unconsciousness. So these things are what I became and sought out. And there were no other adults around who were invested in getting to know me or casting some sunshine my way. And while I always knew a sibling would have brought some joy or distraction, I had none to cling to or cheer me up. My parents both worked jobs they disliked and isolated themselves to opposite sides of the house at night, leaving me alone with television or school work. I have no doubt they loved me, but their own problems and unconsciousness kept them from doing their own self work, which kept them from ever seeing what their dysfunction did to my innocent heart. Their work, their relationship with each other, and thus their relationship with me were all obligations, and I could feel it for eighteen miserable years.

The light that guides me went dark before age ten. From the womb, I was exposed to my mother's misery and disconnection. As a baby, I was affected by my parents' arguing and passive aggressive tactics against one another. These energies were like dark and heavy fingerprints on the bright light of my innocent and trusting soul. From the time I could go to school, I was given a long list of others' expectations for me. I was told when to eat, when to go to the bathroom, and what to learn. No one told me to ask myself or my body what I needed, felt, or knew. No one was interested in what interested me. Eventually, I didn't think I mattered, and no one asked.

Since no one was teaching me how to succeed at life and find peace or purpose, I looked to media and kids at school for guidance on how to be, and I was told "skinny, beautiful, perfect, smiling, and smart." I tried to be these things and lost touch with my heart and soul. What I really wanted to know was how to be loved and seen. I was lacking intimacy of any kind. What could I do to get my parents to want to know me and be with me more? Why did no one seem to be happy to see me? By age three, I had stopped loving myself because no one taught me I was lovable. By six I realized I would get attention for perfect grades in school. By seven I'd discovered stacks of *Playboy* magazines in my parents' closet and figured if I could look like the women in the photos someone would love me. The message was that adults, or men, like and even love women who look like that, and even as an adult, it's hard for me to believe that women who aren't perfect deserve love. This is an example of the broken belief systems parents unknowingly prop up in their children's minds. Now I know someone has to stop and recognize these broken systems for what they are, and the someones are brave and conscious parents like you. While you don't have all the answers yet, you trust your gut that there is a solution for your precious child. And you're so right.

I starved myself by age thirteen, ran for hours on the treadmill, sacrificed sleep to get As while my young brain was growing, and numbed my feelings by staying constantly busy, propelled forward by the school system that promised something (I'm not sure what) at the end.

I did not know happiness until a spiritual awakening and the birth of my first child in my thirties, so I spent decades miserable and many years suicidal. I suffered the kind of neglect that is damaging most children in our society today, and it isn't driven by the drug epidemic or physical abuse. This neglect is largely unconscious, and it is a complete disconnect from the purpose of our existence and relationships. It is an intimacy void and a turning of our backs to the voice of our deepest knowing, our soul, and its plea to remember who we are.

From birth, children look to their parents for everything including what to eat, how to react to stress, how to start their days, and how to fill every minute of their lives. They will do exactly what the caregivers around them do until a cooler or smarter adult shows them a different way, which may or may not be better or safer than what they've learned up to that point. Or at some point, kids learn that the parents have it all wrong and seek answers themselves. I witnessed emotionally immature, inexperienced people who were not in love and who did not know how to seek out or experience joy. I went into the world at eighteen years old knowing only an existence that taught me to focus on achievement and my physical appearance. I was taught to look outside myself, and this is the problem our society is facing with kids. If we want kids to be successful later, happiness and peace are the first objectives we must seek for our kids, and they will only be found by looking within. It's like children are born with magical golden compasses that they can ask questions and follow and trust, but society says, "No, no, don't listen to that compass; take our map instead," only every map is identical and, therefore, cannot possibly serve the unique souls who are so badly in need of conscious and heart-centered guidance. And so we abandon our compass because the parents and the teachers and doctors all agree. "Ignore your intuition," they say, so only children who have completely lost touch with their heart and soul will comply and come out seemingly "normal." I witnessed dozens of seemingly normal kids, and I wondered why I couldn't just submit and find the reality we were offered sufficient. Now I know I was incapable of denying my purpose. Something inside of me was telling me there was more to life. My reality was excruciating, and the message was "keep searching until life feels good," but since it never did, I began wondering if I wanted to live.

My mother had cold, alcoholic parents and lost a twenty-one-year-old brother in a tragic fall from a waterfall when I was eleven-months-old. She was depressed, in constant conflict with my father, and completely overwhelmed with teaching high-needs children; so I witnessed her trying to keep her head above water for eighteen years. From her trials, I learned that life is full of struggle and sadness. She spent most evenings after work resentfully making dinner or reading self-help books in her room (and she did teach me to also love books, so it wasn't all bad). Did she love me? Yes. Could I feel it or understand it? Absolutely not. A parent cannot give from an empty cup, so I therefore received little emotionally from her beyond the few months she breastfed me and the attention I'd receive when I was sick (which was often). When I had my period at age ten, she told me nothing except to not have sex until marriage. I sensed then she didn't have much life experience, and I decided to not ask her any more questions because she likely didn't know much more than me. As a parent, she operated out of obligation and I could feel it in my bones, but the most damaging messages I received from my mother was we don't have control over our circumstances, it's acceptable to be unhappy, and we should just suck it up in life. And I was taught that suffering might just get you some revenge on those who are making you so miserable. All of this was confusing and damaging to me as a child whose natural state was joy and bliss. My bright light was dimmed gradually from birth by the negativity and disconnect around me. Over time, I lost connection with the source of my light and body, and I forgot why I was here.

The only time my anxiety eased some and I could receive the attention I longed for was when I was sick. The stress of school and the pressure to be perfect was put on hold when I was sick. I could stay in bed and watch television, and my mother would bring me food on a tray and drinks with straws. My poor heart wanted love so much that I started trying to make myself sick. I remember licking floors and objects in public hoping I'd catch germs so I could stay home. I can't imagine a more desperate cry for help and love besides an attempt at suicide, and I wouldn't try that for another fifteen years. I also remember jumping off tire swings and high places to try to break my leg and get my parents' attention, and these memories break my heart for the young and innocent me who just wanted to be understood and seen.

My baby-boomer father grew up very poor with lovely, yet young and religious parents and four siblings. So as an adult, he thought if he had a nice house and a corporate career and moved into a suburb with good schools, his job was done, and he had made it. He worked all day at a company he was proud of, came home just in time for dinner, and then watched cable television until he went to bed. If I came in the room and stood in front of the TV to request attention of any kind, I would be waved out of the way. The only thing that would keep him from watching TV and ignoring me was if I needed help with school work or studying for a test, which sounds nice and fatherly, except he helped more for his desired image of having a smart child than for my own well-being because he was taught it's what's on the outside that matters. He didn't know I had a much deeper need than to get an A on a test. He didn't know he was teaching me I didn't matter. Despite his love for me and my few good memories of enjoying music together, he was controlling, threatening, aggressive, dismissive, and completely detached emotionally. He thought I was his to mold and manipulate, and he was like that because it was the way someone parented him. Neglected people neglect people they love because they don't know another way. Abused people abuse people, and abuse can occur even with good intentions. It's time conscious parents start calling out the outdated and abusive parenting advise of past generations–the hitting, threatening, cry-it-out, teach-them-a-lesson nonsense that shatters connection and halts any chance of trust. Looking back, the most damaging message I received from my father was that the airbrushed and visually perfect women in his *Playboy* magazines were worthy of his attention and time. This broken belief system would cause me tremendous trouble and pain, and I would be nearly forty before I would break its hold on me.

My evolved self knows this inability to connect, selfishness, and unconsciousness goes back generations. It is not my parents' fault they did not have the self-awareness or courage to break the cycle. Breaking cycles is painful and hard, and it is easier to stay asleep. My parents loved me, as all parents do. Love and neglect can coexist, however, and children are precious and vulnerable and can be deeply damaged during their first few years. I looked for attention and love in many places after not finding any at home. I felt separate from people and always an outsider, even among friends or groups at school, and to this day I feel surprised when people enjoy my company. My parents didn't have close relationships with their siblings outside of holidays, and they had few friends outside of work, none of whom came around or offered me any positive guidance or support. I remember having excruciating emotions, having had no one modeling useful coping, self-love, or self-care regimens. Now I know I was and am an empath, meaning I can feel the emotions of others along with my own, which can be confusing and painful for a child or adult. Not having anyone to define these things for me or teach me how to cope, I was angry and emotional a lot as a young person, and my feelings for my parents turned from indifference, to hurt, to anger. I spent almost no time with them after the age of twelve. By thirteen, I was given beer on a spring break trip I took with a friend and her negligent mother, and I immediately loved how the alcohol allowed me to escape my pain, which had been so constant I didn't know it wasn't normal.

Now I know this escape was my consciousness leaving my body, which was a much-needed break after thirteen years of feeling the emotions of my unhappy and unconscious parents. I drank and over-exercised and made near straight As through high school, and I don't remember one happy moment at home. The saddest part was I didn't know any genuinely happy people, so I didn't even miss it. I just didn't understand the point of life. Life was hard and hurt deeply, and the adults in my life had no information. They, as I know now, were worse off than I was because they stayed asleep. I was determined to make sense of it, even if it killed me.

College was more of the same with the secret misery, over-exercising, drinking, and starving myself. I figured I'd discover the point of it all in a relationship, so I dated and slept with boys and girls and then more boys, with a desperation I can still recall. I wanted love and acceptance and for someone to invest in me. My parents didn't see or appreciate the real me, so surely someone out there would. First, they'd see how perfect I was physically, and then they'd grow to love me. I lacked intimacy of any kind with my family of origin. And looking back now with a lens of compassion and love, I now know I was trying every way I knew to find it. The passion and drive I came into life with had been long-diminished. I had stopped mentioning ballet, writing, traveling, music, and low-paying dreams like the Peace Corps because my father said I'd never make any money or I was too smart to be a teacher or not good enough to be a ballerina. He didn't know these dreams were whispers of my soul, and to this day I am nothing but a dancer in my dreams. And so I listen to every word my four-year-old says and take her very seriously when she says she needs a suit to go to space. All that matters is she listens to the words of her soul, and we have to remind children to keep doing this even as broken systems tell them to conform and mute their intuitions and connections to the universe, or Source. Look inside, I tell my daughter, because she is the expert on her time here.

I took my communications and English degrees, which were as close to dance and foreign language as I could grasp, and I taught and wrote for industries I did not like and hated my life. Twice I took all the prescription pills in my house after fights with people I loved and ended up hospitalized and treated for depression, eating disorders, and alcohol abuse. No one I'd met could tell me why I should keep on struggling and keep on not finding peace and love. Finally, nearly ten years after finishing college, as my daughter's bright light was preparing to choose me, I enrolled in the yoga teacher training I'd always dreamed of doing. Yoga was a substitution for dance, and I'd been hooked since I was nineteen in college. I was led to a spiritual training in San Diego by the first soul friend I'd ever made, and I spent five hundred hours in all learning about spirituality and the God, the Source, that is left when religion and dogma and ego are stripped away. On one of the first days of training, I did a chakra clearing meditation and saw and felt things I had never felt and had never heard explained. At the age of thirty-three (which happens to be a deeply transformational and spiritual age), I received the information and tools that saved my life and taught me to look within. Suddenly, I felt the same connection I'd felt as a child when I prayed or watched the stars out of my bedroom window with warm tears flowing down my cheeks. The answers were all within, and I had been so uncomfortable and confused for decades, and every adult I'd ever looked to for guidance said the opposite. "I didn't know," I remember saying to myself during the meditation. Warm tears ran down my face once more, and I suddenly had all the information I needed to never want to die again. And this information is in the pages of this book.

I know that without the principles I discuss in this book, I would have died by now. And I know that had someone taught me these things when I was a child, I would have known to trust and love myself first. I would have known the difference in how my body feels during chaos and during peace and what to do to restore balance. Most importantly, I'd know about peace, joy, and compassion–the three things we are on this planet to experience and share and the three things I want for my children. I want them for all the children in this world but especially for the struggling ones who are likely here to wake up the rest of the population who is still asleep.

I always wished I had a sibling to laugh with or chime in when things were especially dark. But then my training would have been cut short. I needed those specific circumstances. I needed that particular darkness with my parents at that time so I could later saturate the planet with the opposite—with the brightest, strongest light that would save children and restore love in many people's hearts. I can't wait for you to say to someone you love, with tears streaming down your cheeks, "I didn't know."

I know I needed to experience the dark in this lifetime to be reborn as a minister of light, but there are jobs that need to be done that don't require this devastation. Every time I help a parent remember who they are and where they're going, I'm saving at least one member of their family from wandering in the dark until they die or take their own life. Instead, I work to keep children ignited from birth and centered in their divine purpose so they can get to work bringing light to our planet in many beautiful ways, without the detour.

Chapter 3:

TAKE BACK YOUR POWER

My recommendation for helping your child with his emotions is scientific, yet it might seem spiritual. I'm sure you've heard of experiments like the ones with house plants where one grows in a room with a recording of "I hate you" being repeated over and over, and one grows in a room with "I love you." One eventually dies from being inundated with dark energy, and one thrives from the constant flow of love. IKEA, brilliantly, recently did an anti-bullying campaign where one plant is bullied with recorded comments like "no one likes you" and one is encouraged and complimented. It's stunning to see the wilted and defeated plant in the end that has been bullied. The same experiment has been done with one plant "listening" to Metallica and the other to Mozart. Which do you think thrived? My point is these experiments seem silly, yet their results have been repeated over and over. There are hundreds of YouTube videos on the subject and many on a similar experiment where two jars of water or rice sit sealed for months next to each other. On one is written the word "hate" and on the other, you guessed it, "love." After weeks the jar of water with the dark message literally becomes darker, and the jar with the "lighter" message remains clearer and freer of yucky debris. After months the difference is shocking. The hate jar of water has been almost completely taken over by dark slime, while the love jar is still so free of debris that light can shine through.

We can think of our newborn babies like squeaky clean glass jars with sparkling clear water inside. Of course, no baby will be born into an extreme like all light or all dark all the time. But what if everything a baby hears as it grows by its family and its society was given a score on this dark/light continuum, and we could witness the subtle changes that don't seem significant until years have gone by and yucky debris has blocked out all the light? What if the jars of water in the experiment had other, less extreme words like "indifferent," "happy," "mediocre," "bad," "shame" written on them? All words would make a difference, however small, toward light or dark, and eventually one would win. Maybe a jar becomes just murky and sluggish for life while another stays clear for several more years before becoming over-come by grimy darkness. If you think about it, you can probably pick people you know who have very dirty glass jars. You can feel it even if you can't see it, and it probably feels not-so-great to them as well.

Clearly, living things are affected by their surround-ings, even plants who are thought to be nonsentient, and the explanation is purely scientific. Sound can be healing or harmful. Sound waves come at you and they can relax, inspire, excite, or wrap you in a loving hug. But they can also stab you like daggers, and there are many sounds in between. Perhaps Metallica hits our bodies like "I'm so angry" or "I hate you," and individual reactions depend on each person's experience. I could make it sound woo-woo, but really it's science. If you look at every sound, thought, person, object, and action as having a charge–positive or negative, dark, or light–or a score between love and hate, you can see why it's helpful to play beau-tiful music and think of each thought as sending off a bomb or a bouquet of flowers. Each positive word takes our day up a notch and gives us a positive point, while each negative word pulls us down. This is why I some-times break into made-up songs of "love, love, love, I'm calling for love, love, love" when someone in our home is upset or I'm struggling myself. I take control of the situation and pull my easiest and fastest tool out of my hat. And my kids love it. They can feel the energy improving, and they are grateful to me for taking charge, leading the way back to balance, and teaching them a simple yet effective skill. "You have power" is the message I'm teaching them. And "no situation is too far gone to rescue because we can start again."

Our Scattered Attention

Try something: close your eyes and think about the last time you were at the beach or a lake and stood on the sand with the waves moving over your feet. In other words, pretend you are at the beach with your toes in the sand. Use your imagination. The longer you think about it, the more detail you can recall or create. Maybe you can remember how the water felt or looked. Perhaps you remember the seagulls, the hot sand, or the sensation of your feet sinking into the sand as the water rushed back. With your imagination, you can almost be there now. Next imagine the kitchen where you grew up. With your eyes closed, can you picture it? Can you feel or hear any details? What color are the walls? Who is present?

Everyone has varying abilities to imagine "in their heads," but we do this–we go somewhere else–all the time. Just from that quick exercise, you now have left bits of you at the beach and at your childhood home. And if you were scared of the ocean or had a traumatic experience in your childhood home, these were not safe places for you to linger. "How does this help my child?" you ask. It is hugely beneficial for children to learn to bring their attention and energy back into their own body (this is called grounding, and you'll learn all about it in later chapters). My purpose here is to teach you, the caregiver, that we are energy (or light) and can affect our lives in both positive and negative ways by learning to take our energy to other places and also to bring it all back.

Now pretend you can't find your keys. You're tearing your house apart and going nuts because you are late. You finally sit on the couch, frustrated, and decide to call an Uber. As you sit there, dazed, waiting for a ride, your mind wanders and you suddenly remember using your keys to unlock your garage's back door the previous night in the rain, something you normally don't do. You see for a moment the keys still in the lock outside and you smack your palm to your forehead. For those ten seconds while you were thinking back to the last time you saw the keys, your attention was on the keys and was not present in your body looking at your nails or checking out your new boots, for example. While you were going over your last eighteen hours in your mind your attention went to several places in time and space– your desk at work, the drive home, bringing the garbage cans back from the curb to the garage, finding the garage door down, and walking quickly in the rain around the garage to the back. And when you finally saw the keys in your mind still in the lock, you said, "Oh, yeah!" which brought your attention back to your body and the room you were in, and you ran outside to grab your keys.

Now close your eyes and go back to the beach. Imagine someone walking up to you and handing you a cold drink. You cannot truly imagine this and also be thinking about your nails in the present. Now, keeping your eyes closed, go back to your childhood kitchen. Someone is cooking at the stove? You can bounce back and forth. Kitchen. Beach. Keys dangling in the rain. Kitchen. Beach. Keys. Where your attention is, you are. Whoa, whoa, you thought the only place you can be is where your body is. Again, the explanation is science. Quantum physics in fact. While in your childhood kitchen in your mind, you are obviously there without your body, and this is why it's not clear in the physical ways you're used to. You don't see your old kitchen as clearly as you see your hands in front of your face because you're using your brain alone while back in your parents' kitchen to do things like perceive your surroundings, which is something our society does not teach us we can do. Back in the kitchen without your physical eyeballs, you have to just observe while imagining and wait for your brain to make discoveries. All of this is called visualization, and it can be a miraculous tool in healing. For example, if my child is nervous about something at school, we can visualize things going our way the night before or by taking a few moments before leaving the house. We can go ahead of ourselves to our day and prepare the space for our highest and best good. While ideas like these are not mainstream, we are more than capable of affecting our lives through visualization, and many of my clients are surprised at how receptive their children are to these tools.

When I go to my own childhood kitchen in my mind, I remember and can almost feel the hard and cold tile floors. I can remember the textures of the wooden cabinets and plastic cabinet knobs, and I can see outside to the porch and yard. I know I cannot focus on seeing the yard of my childhood home and being in the room my physical body is in at the same time. If I look out the window in my current physical reality, I can alternate between seeing it and seeing my childhood kitchen window, but I cannot do both. Typically we just call this "thinking about our childhood kitchen" or daydreaming. When we think about it, when we think of things while we daydream, we do "go there," which is why people clap their hands in front of us when we're zoned out and say, "Hello? Where were you just now?" When we daydream, we are literally leaving our bodies and placing our attention somewhere far away from our physical body, and this is the first principle in this book that will help explain how all people, especially children, benefit from learning to bring all their attention back into their bodies.

Now we know we leave some of our attention behind when we jump from place to place in our minds. A similar thing happens when you think of a person. Let's assume each person is living inside a round, glass fishbowl filled with whatever good or bad experiences and emotions they've taken on in their life so far. When you think of them, you briefly go into their fishbowl for that split second, and you can catch whatever they are feeling. If the person is happy and likes you, you probably won't experience any ill effects, but if the person is dealing with heavy emotions or has reason to think negatively about you, you can end up taking on their feelings. This is important for children because many of the emotions they feel are not their own. Once this is understood, a child can be taught to clear his personal space, in addition to bringing his attention back into his body.

In middle school, at least once a week I'd call my best friend, and she'd say, "Oh my goodness, I had my hand on the phone to call you! You must be psychic!" And it happened the other way around just as often. I know this has happened to you and a friend or relative. You hadn't talked to your college roommate in five years, and when you text she says she had a dream about you last night. My father's generation would say "what a coincidence!" but our brain–our consciousness–is not bound to our physical bodies. It thinks of someone and quickly goes over and taps them, without meaning to and without knowing it's doing it. It's energy. We're all energy. Popping over and tapping your college roomie is one thing because you want to talk to her, but if you're mad at your neighbor and think about him every five minutes throughout the entire day, you're definitely not sending rainbows back and forth. The frustration and anger you're feeling when you're ruminating over something negative are caused by you feeling other people's emotions. Our brains are that powerful. And now that we recognize this happens, we can use our powerful brain to stop it and even prevent it.

Browser Overload

When I first got an iPhone, I had no idea the internet app opened a new window for each website. After a few weeks, my new phone became slower until someone heard me complaining about it at a bar. The bartender came over and double-clicked my home button, showing me how to close the one hundred or more windows I had opened at once. I didn't know that every time I opened a new website, it was being drained by the other ninety-nine open windows. The overload was slowing my hardware, and in turn making me frustrated. The delay affected my ability to email my boss, and my texts wouldn't come in for minutes or sometimes hours. Every day I experienced the overload, I felt worse because it was affecting my ease and flow.

So what if when we open our eyes in the morning it is like opening an internet browser? First, perhaps you open a window to think about the FedEx package that was supposed to be delivered yesterday, and oh no, what if someone stole it on the porch overnight. A piece of yourself is now mad at FedEx and perhaps your husband for distracting you. Next, a meeting at your child's school that you're anxious about. Now that worrisome situation is occupying a second opened window. You've sent a bit of yourself to the school to sit and worry until the meeting. Next, you think about the neighbor with an RV parked in front of his house because you can hear your husband in the next room on the phone with the homeowners' association. The problem neighbor becomes a third open window, and your physical body's battery goes from 95 percent to 90 percent. By noon you have sixteen windows open, you're frustrated that you haven't accomplished more in your morning, and you can't stop thinking about your problem neighbor. You also feel anxious and can't shake the anger you feel about a $400 iTunes bill your eleven-year-old racked up by ordering movies and music albums he listens to only once. By dinnertime you snap at your middle son, and it's all uphill from there to bedtime. Let's just say that every new window you open, you leave a small part of your split attention there. You literally spread yourself thin with every scattered worry. Now if we were jumping from thought to thought pumping ourselves up and sending encouragement to our problems, we wouldn't be so drained, but as humans it's our nature to worry and ruminate. When we visited the beach, a sliver of the attention you need to read this book was left behind. Thankfully the beach is a good place to visit, so you may not be in a hurry to bring back your beach self who's being soothed by the waves. But your pissed-at-the-neighbor self is spinning her wheels and wasting energy. It's like you left a version of yourself out in the road by the neighbor's RV, and she is still out there waiting for a fight. If your attention is split into mostly distressing windows all day, you'll have the same number of yourselves left behind and distressed.

The solution is remembering, "Shoot! I have so many windows open! No wonder I'm feeling anxious and short-tempered." It's purposely going and closing all the windows, just like we do with our laptops and phones. Suddenly our phones can hold a charge and aren't freezing. If we treat our challenges like those houseplants and whisper good wishes, encouragement, and ask for the best outcome for all involved, the version of you that's looking for a fight in your yoga pants out in the cul-de-sac will suddenly be enlightened with a new perspective and choose a new way. If we imagine being physically disconnected from the conflicts that bring us stress using the power of our imagination (which is not make-believe, despite what we were taught), we will experience relief in a variety of subtle and then eventually more drastic ways. It's like every time we take our attention somewhere new, we cast a fishing line out to the situation or person. With intention we can bring our pieces back to ourselves by closing our tabs, recalling our fishing lines, and bringing closure by sending our best wishes.

And what do you think will happen to your personal fishbowl when the RV neighbor sends you a scathing email? His nasty words will be like gross fingerprints on the outside of your glass. Perhaps a phrase he uses reminds you of your alcoholic father, and you splinter into a memory from age twelve. In this case, your anger is not your own. You are unconsciously seeing and feeling the angry emotions of your neighbor, and you are not used to being angry. So the interaction with him makes you feel terrible. Your solution is to realize you've been slimed by someone thinking negatively about you. He thought something negative about your new pool construction noise or the fact you've only lived there for six years, and he's been in the neighborhood since the '70s, and his fishing lure nailed you. What if tomorrow when you wake you have a plan to protect yourself? This plan and much more can be found in chapter six.

In the same way we climb into the hot bath after a long day with work and family to wash away the grime and soak away the stress, we must call back our scattered bits of self and disconnect from people's thoughts and energies. We can learn to remove the sticky fingerprints people leave on our personal fishbowls. We can dislodge the fishing lures people cast and snag into us, and we can strain out the yucky debris that others leave behind in our otherwise peaceful waters. And once you realize what a spectacular tool our brain is in cleaning and protecting ourselves, you'll be dropping everything to teach your kids.

***

My program is broken down into five universal principles, which I am packaging for parents and kids. These principles are not my own but have been brought to me by angels, both seen and unseen, and have been taught for thousands of years by prophets like Jesus Christ, Buddha, Krishna, Mohammad, Lao Tzu, and others who simply want us to realize our power and remember we are all one. This power, I believe, lies in our brains and is accessible to everyone at any time, using tools you already own. In summary, we were meant to know that we too can perform what most consider miracles. If this makes you uncomfortable, I challenge you to read on for the sake of your child, who needs this information more than you can imagine. Your child can teach a friend, continuing to spread this good news like wildfire. What if by reading this book you will save a young person's life? Listen to the small voice within that says all this sounds strangely familiar.

The Five Principles

1. The first principle, which explains we are all energy, will introduce you to a reason for living that makes your existence make sense, and you'll realize your significance and connection to other people and the world. Remember where we came from and connect to our Source, which is very much a subject of science. Kids need to hear that they are here for a special purpose, and once you confirm it for them, they can get to work remembering why they are here. I've never been more excited or more "on fire" (as my spiritual teacher says) as when I learned about my special purpose. It was the news my soul had been waiting thirty-three years to hear.

2. The second principle will help you discover your greatest superpower–your ability to create–and help you see that like an artist with one hundred colors of paint to choose from, you have the ability to paint your day any way you want it. We are, in fact, marvelous creators, starting with decisions we make when we wake and intentions we set as we get our household ready for the day, meaning we can affect outcomes and reverse bad days with saying so, seeing what we want, and sending only positive versions of ourselves out into the world. This principle is a

simplification of the law of attraction and will let kids know they are like wizards, telling the universe what they want and then experiencing it delivering that to them. For me, the universe was the first place I found unwavering strength and support.

3. The third principle is good news and shows how we are in charge of our personal bubble or fishbowl. The first step to solving a problem–or removing debris from our fishbowl that is bringing us drama or uncomfortable emotion–is realizing we've been invaded. The fishbowl you reside in can be affected by other people and by words and thoughts, including our own. You have power over this space, can command its clearing, and can invite in whatever you want most in your life. My fishbowl visualization, which you will learn in chapter six, works great with children and teens (and parents!), and it teaches us to clear personal space. Sometimes after I teach them the fishbowl exercise, clients will experience their own energy for the first time in their life, and it is a glorious feeling to finally realize your dark and painful emotions are not your own.

4. The fourth principle teaches that you can fill your cup physically and emotionally using our two sources above and below. It arms you

with easily accessible tools that reduce anxiety and help us realize the gifts the Earth offers freely. What I call my "earth tools" are some of my most effective strategies, often because children are unknowingly deprived of earth energies, and the smallest dose makes an unbelievable difference.

5. The fifth principle tells you about our team, our entourage, who was assigned to us at birth and never leaves us, and it also warns of unhelpful energies that will interfere with us and drain our batteries if we let them. Most are beings like angels and guides who are, despite what it seems, very scientific in nature, as they are energy or light and not people with wings like we've been told. The concept of "my guides" has helped numerous children return to school and activities they love simply because the method works and brings the child power, peace, and comfort. We'll also learn about the support of loved ones who aren't in a body but who can act as guardians and protectors, and finally we'll learn to protect ourselves from the unhelpful energies.

Applying the Principles with Your Child

How will all this help my struggling child who hates school? Your child is a special kind of soul who feels emotions stronger than older people and more so than many kids his age, but the emotions he's feeling are not his own. It's not his fault, and it's certainly no fault of his family. He needs to know the truth about his source, his personal space, the energy around him, and the power of his brain to access places our physical senses cannot detect. These principles are supported by multiple religions and have been time-tested. These principles saved my life and will save the lives of millions of children, maybe your own. A voice inside has whispered for some time that there must be something more, and this book is the answer for which you've been waiting. Your suspicion that your child's uniqueness is not a problem, but a gift, is correct. I'm excited you've found this book!

Chapters four through eight each contain an explanation of the five principles that can bring you and your child emotional peace. You will learn my personal experience with each, along with a simple explanation, and a tool to begin practicing right away.

Tools That Accompany Each Principle

Affirmation: Repeat these throughout your day. They are easy to remember so you can repeat them while driving and pull them out when your "human" or ego gets in your way. Your subconscious is recording your every word. Tell it and the universe what you want at every opportunity.

Visualization: You are a creator. See it. Believe it. Receive it. We will learn to use our imaginations to get what we want and affect change in our and our families' lives.

Chapter 4:

YOU ARE LIGHT

"Don't you know yet? It is your light
that lights the world."
– Rumi

grew up going to a Christian church occasionally. I really liked the music, and I know now it was because I could feel the high vibration of the music. If they played Metallica, for example, I would not have had the same reaction. Music in church is played with the intention of praising God (or Source), the highest and most positive energy, right up there with the words "I love you." I could feel the contrast of that feeling compared to how it felt at home. Sometimes they used bells, and I remember thinking they sounded like angels. The music had a high vibration, and my young self just knew it felt good. I did not like Sunday school very much because the stories didn't make sense and were a little scary. The only time I felt a connection to (what I was taught was called) God was when I prayed alone in my head at bedtime with my hands clasped and my legs curled into fetal position. I would desperately ask for help and felt "held," in a way I couldn't describe at the time. Since no one else was talking about talking directly to God, I kept my relationship with "Him" private. My mother taught me the Lord's Prayer, but as a child the words meant little, although I appreciate it was the only spiritual tool she could offer me.

The stories depicting God as a man are not helpful or true. God is what all of us are when we aren't in a body, what we will be when we leave our current bodies: Light. Energy. Electricity. All of which never die. They're eternal. While each of us individually is light, God (or Source) is all the light there ever was combined– the entire universe before it broke off a piece of itself in order to learn and evolve. Similarly, this is what we do when we have children, whether it's our plan or not: we reproduce these physical bodies that then hold their gorgeous light, and through these children we are forced to learn and evolve. They are our teachers if we listen and let them be themselves. I think all parents agree that without your child(ren), you would be a completely different person, and probably a less evolved one. There is no doubt children bring countless blessings, and some of these blessings are challenges that once overcome, will allow us to be more conscious and fulfilled.

It Turns Out Science Is Spiritual

The way our consciousness moved through time and space in chapter three from our new boots on the couch, to the beach, to our childhood kitchen, to our lost keys, and back to our couch resembles the behavior of only one element: electricity. What matter can jump around and travel time and place? None. You are light, and this is valuable and freeing information to many kids who struggle to find purpose in our world that places so much importance on the external and material. These kids need to know that they are special and powerful and that there are others who feel the same and have survived and thrived. There is so much hope. Once this concept is explained, my hope is you'll look at your own life, as well as your child's, in a different, well, light.

It turns out all the religious God talk is not as out there as it seems because God–and every one of us–is light! He doesn't have a beard, and he is not judging you. If God is not a man because he isn't in a body and doesn't physically look like anything at all and is in fact not a he, then what is God? I call him God and use the pronoun "he" only because that was the only original creator anyone discussed when I was growing up. My paternal grandfather was a Southern Baptist minister, and there was a great deal of religious exposure with him and my grandmother, all of which was positive. They were my greatest sources of joy and love, and their presence in my life must have been planned. Without them, I may have fallen down a much darker path. I know now that there is just one original energy, and I don't care what religion or modality gets you to understand him, as long as you find peace and purpose in the end.

God is the original consciousness of our entire universe, of which we don't have much more than the slightest understanding. You know when the woo woos say, "We are One"? (I used to roll my eyes, too.) This is what they're talking about. Instead of delving into some very heavy science, let's just say that in the beginning (an unimaginably long time ago) there was nothing but God. In fact, let's call him the creator of all things, or Source. There were no planets or galaxies or gardens of Eden. The creator of all things was alone and peaceful as if in a meditation, and he was just light, an electricity we cannot fathom. He was everything, and he was perfect. He had all he needed, and without duality like a planet or a physical body, there was nothing but bliss. He was what many people who have had near-death or out-of-body experiences talk about: an unbelievable peace and comfort, pure love.

Then like the first man to invent a deep diving suit to experience the depths of the ocean, the creator of all things created objects, very small and simple at first, and sent pieces of himself into the objects to experience something new. He realized he couldn't really experience his bliss and perfection unless he knew the opposite and spent time in the middle ground. He sought contrast. He recognized that duality was required to truly explore and know all the complexities of existence. And so the creator of all things made one thing first, perhaps a small rock, and he sent a sliver of his consciousness to experience that rock in the form of a little organism of some kind. And source experienced life. That organism evolved as all organisms do, and as it reproduced, the creator of all things put a second piece of his consciousness into it. Now the creator of everything was in three places at once. Do you agree that his two new creations are still him? Are the three of them not *one* being? Eventually, he experienced many existences at once, gaining new and unique perspectives and becoming better at appreciating the pure bliss and love that was his natural state. When one of the organisms' bodies died, that slice of consciousness–its light–would leave the physical body and return to its source, still the same just not within physical state anymore. And every time the same slice of Source would go into a body and die and return, it would gain wisdom, having a new experience and overcoming a challenge, however small.

A million years later, Source had billions and billions of creations. And if somehow all his creations' physical bodies all died at once, they'd all be reunited, and Source would have found himself alone again in his perfect bliss and love. By now planets and solar systems have been created and destroyed as life evolved, searching for the perfect circumstances to create more complex life. Eventually the dinosaurs would come and go on Earth, and finally, humans would make their debut. The human brain was so powerful it made humans the first sentient creature, at least on Earth, that experienced emotions. And thus began all of humanity's struggle with the countless emotions that drive all our drama and stress. The human brain is so complex and powerful, humans can feel the emotions of others, communicate without speaking, travel through time and space using their minds, and heal their bodies and energy fields. But people have only known about these powers for certain periods of time on Earth. This good news is what Jesus the Christ (more about him later), and many other prophets, came into physical form to tell humans. And they all came at times in history where love hadn't been defined, and their light was badly needed.

Great News, Even for Atheists

And today as we approach 2020, it's definitely a dark, yet exciting, time on the planet Earth. Most people are asleep in that they are unconscious of the things they cannot see with their eyeballs. They have forgotten they are a slice of our Source, God, and they are having children and teaching them to also be asleep, which is catastrophic for thousands of highly evolved children who are susceptible to the dark energies of depression, bullying, drugs, alcohol, violence, and suicide. Like me, being kept from the knowledge of my true nature was life-threatening. I had no reason to live if God wasn't real and we just turned into dirt when we died. I was desperate for good news–to learn that I wasn't separate from and unworthy of the universe, that I was a part of it and had access to every miracle. Imagine if when your child played a video game, he or she became so immersed in the avatar they chose to represent them that they forgot they were sitting on a couch holding a controller. They forget about the portion of themselves that isn't in the video game and cannot remember their parents (their source) or the soccer game and birthday party they have planned later in the day (their purpose for the time). This is what happens to most souls once they enter a physical human body.

Way before the age of thirty, I needed to know that every time one of the first people on Earth was born, our Source, the mother ship of energy, would send down a slice of consciousness–a soul–that would light a flame in the physical form and occupy the human to experience duality and learn about the other end of the love spectrum. The Earth is like a schoolhouse for our perfect and bright souls. After several thousands of years of humans walking the earth, the same lights would occupy multiple physical bodies over multiple lifetimes. Families would come into physical form again and again together to experience more complex challenges, and some souls would go down and help other souls they love. And I'm telling you all this because this information is a game changer! We are not here to check off to-do lists and struggle. We are here for a divine and exciting purpose, and we chose our families to challenge us and evolve together. Your child needs this information. And as outlandish as all this sounds, it is more realistic than a story about a man in the sky with a beard who judges and punishes us when we make mistakes. My explanation is science, which is the most straightforward way I can explain these principles. Most atheists think they're too smart to believe stories about men in the sky, but to believe we are just animals who live once briefly and are then snuffed out like a candle the moment the physical body expires drastically underestimates the power and eternity of a soul. Your soul. Your child's soul. And all of this is true even if you don't believe, and even if you think I'm nuts.

Maybe you last lived in a human body in the 1800s or maybe you last died in World War II. Many of us occupied a human when the knowledge of our power was more widely believed and taught, like in the legendary days of Atlantis or when Jesus the Christ was teaching his disciples how to perform miracles (if these parts of history fascinate you as they do me, I suggest checking out the *Bible Speaks* books by Marisa and Joseph Moris). But as you can imagine, power like this in groups threatened many rulers and religious men throughout human history, which is likely how Jesus found himself on the cross. This knowledge about the power of our brains has been wiped out of human memory and out of most written record out of fear–to take away people's power and to keep us dependent and compliant–but today more and more people are waking up and reconnecting with their inner light and potential. The Earth is also evolving, as all living beings are, and humans are being ushered into a new and exciting time. All people, even the atheists, can now feel energy, when before they felt nothing, and it's driving people, especially parents, to ask questions. "What if there is more?" they ask. And the unique children like yours who struggle know there is more, though they obviously can't articulate it, and will be relieved when they find out they're right.

For the people who could already feel energy, like your child, well they've begun feeling so much that they'll be forced to learn about and master the powers their brains are begging them to use. And if we stay in the knowledge of our light, being conscious of the connection we have with all living beings, we start to remember how to access these larger, more powerful parts of our brain. An atom is 99.9 percent energy and only 0.1 percent matter. We've evolved to the point where even the smartest, most skeptical atheists are starting to consider deeper, less tangible possibilities. "I'll believe it when I see it" is now the declaration of simple and three-dimensional thinking, and our children will suffer under limited belief systems such as these. There is so much more beyond what our eyes and ears tell us, and I dream of a generation who accepts concepts like telepathy and self-healing as willingly as we accept communicating with our voices and Western medicine today.

This Little Light of Mine

If we tell children that they are light and ask them to tell us why they're here, what their bodies say they need, and how to solve problems (perhaps even huge ones in ways no adult would ever imagine!), we'll be delighted when they grow into self-aware, self-soothing, and self-confident young adults who know where they're going in life and are, most importantly, happy. In today's society these types of young adults are less and less common because, for the most part, we've steered children outside of themselves from birth, and we've been doing it for decades. As a child, I became so disconnected from my own wants and needs that I didn't know how to exist without having my physical and academic accomplishments validated by someone outside of me. I needed directions to follow so I could receive an A and be told I was excellent, while the C students were only average. When asked what I wanted I would look to someone else for answers about myself because I'd been taught I knew nothing, while I was in fact a part of *everything*. I just had to wait a long time to meet a conscious or awake adult who was willing to invest in me and tell me about my light, my connection to all other humans, and my divine right to remember and step into my special purpose.

Eventually, I learned when we are not in a body (and die), we return to the mother ship of our source, and we wait in bliss with every soul we've ever loved for eternity until everyone together (the universal consciousness) decides there is another circumstance on Earth for us to learn and evolve. Then a pair of humans is chosen to conceive that soul, the soul investigates to make sure the circumstance is still ideal for its own growth, and it then waits while the bun is in the oven. (This is a good time to let you know that if a miscarriage happens, the same soul that is waiting can just wait for another body or another pregnancy.) Then the miraculous moment the baby is born, Source sends down a little slice of its consciousness that you name and wrap up in a little blanket. The baby–the body–becomes the avatar for your light to play in a video game, otherwise known as life on Earth. The trick is helping the baby stay aware of its light starting at birth. If a child is born into an unconscious and of-the-world household, its chances of staying close to its light and divine connection are slim. But what if parents were told about their child's light instead of given advice from broken belief systems like "babies don't feel pain," or "don't spoil that baby," and "let him cry it out." For at that moment when the baby is born and put into the parents' arms, who do you think is more in touch with his/her light? With his/her divine purpose and with God? A baby has been with Source, with God, way more recently than we have. Shouldn't we ask what he/she remembers and needs from us? Shouldn't we wait for kids to reveal themselves to us and follow their leads? Shouldn't we trust their lights, which act as golden compasses in their hearts, guiding them and protecting them in the form of intuition and discernment?

I feel like I was lowered into a dark well four decades ago, and after thirty-three years a person who has just been sunbathing is lowered down, all smiling and warm and happy, talking about the sun, sunset and sunrise. Who am I to lecture this sun goddess about the sun? How could I possibly know anything about the sun, having been at the bottom of a dark well for thirty-three years? When both of my babies were born, I assumed they were the wisest and most grounded, happiest creatures alive, certainly the happiest I'd ever met. I assumed I knew them before. They had been my most cherished grand-mother or the sister I lost in a house fire or the enemy soldier I shot with a bow and arrow three thousand years ago in a battle over fresh water for our villages. I'm coming on strong with the woo here, but can you honestly tell me you didn't feel the light when your children were born? How fresh and satisfied and present they were? A light that bright doesn't just come out of nowhere in your womb. A light that powerful doesn't just go out when the body doesn't work anymore. A light like that has been lit for eons. A light like that came here for a reason. I want to be that voice for my children that says, "I see your light, and together we'll help you remember your light no matter how much darkness the world throws at you."

Our Inner Compass

The corner of society I was raised in said one of two things. Either you should be an atheist because you are too smart to believe anything you cannot see with your own eyes like men in the sky, or you should believe in a man-made religion's explanation of creation and human purpose that instills fear and has a codified history and set of rules full of inconsistencies. Later in life I'd learn that the Bible was written by many people at many different times in history, almost all after Jesus the Christ even walked the Earth. While I do believe religious texts were written with divine inspiration and reveal many universal truths and clues toward finding the meaning in life, I receive the most wisdom by listening to my innermost teacher, my light, which is directly connected to Source above and can link me with the all-knowing collective consciousness. This means I have access to the wisdom of the universe if I believe I do and can find the stillness and silence to hear it.

Maybe your children were your parent or sibling in a previous human experience. Maybe your problem neighbor with the RV was someone you've had conflict with before. The point is our beginning and end is not determined by these bodies we're occupying, but most people are aware of only their human, or physical body. Our humans get hungry and grouchy and argue with partners over laundry and with teens over iTunes bills. But once we realize we are light and the reason we are here is to learn and evolve through overcoming obstacles and attempting to spread love, we begin to see how inconsequential most of what upsets us is. Thinking life begins and ends with this body I'm in sat so poorly with my soul, and many young people are confused like this. Before I found teachers who could explain this stuff in words that spoke to my soul, I had trouble finding purpose in staying alive. If life was a lot of sadness and struggle and we just die someday, any day, and turn into dirt, what is the point in fighting or getting out of bed in the morning? I obviously wanted to live, and I fought my way back from attempted suicide several times, even though little changed with my depression. Ultimately, the cure for my depression was finding out I was light. I found out my light was so bright I could spread it out wide and clear my bedroom. I could puff it up strong like a coat of armor on my way into a stressful situation and ask Source above to protect me. I could wrap it around me like a quilt my grandmother sewed in the 1970s, while asking the universe for comfort. And I could send it ahead of me to flights that made me anxious or days that seem overwhelming. And I could teach all this to my kids!

I think about my eight-year-old self and wish she knew she could send her light ahead of her. She could wrap it around herself when she was hopeless on the school bus or feeling the energy of the bus driver's argument with her spouse. She could find comfort in it when she was crying alone in bed at night. And she could have used it to keep her personal space clear. She could have removed her parents' negative emotions and stale, stuck energy from herself. Then she could do the same with kids at school who were bullies because they themselves were bullied at home. She would then have been able to distinguish her emotions from those around her. She would have known she wasn't broken, or unwanted, or alone. She would have embodied her true identity–light–and been affected and fooled less by the darkness around her.

Our lights and their power are my first principle, and I have an exercise to help you harness your light and bring you–all of you–back into your body. This is what the woo-woos would call grounding, and it is bringing all your attention, your light, and your consciousness back into your physical human body. It's consciously and with intention being present. It's bringing your attention back from the beach, your childhood kitchen, and your missing keys. As my first spiritual teacher's teacher said, it's feeling your butt in your chair.

Affirmation to become you and only you:

"I am now [your name] and only [your name]. I am my real and whole self now." Say this when you enter or leave crowds or are experiencing stress.

"I command anything that is not mine to leave now and be recycled into the one true Source."

Visualization to gather your attention and reunite your energies:

With your eyes closed imagine your light in your chest. If you can't imagine a light, then just hold your hands to your chest, trusting it's there. Next, see if you can bring this light (or just your attention) up to your forehead. Keeping your attention on your head, say

"I'm calling back all of my scattered pieces. Come back." And just witness what happens. You might see or feel something filling you back up. You may feel nothing. There is no wrong answer. Either way, know that your intention has made it happen. You are now gathered because you commanded it to be so.

Chapter 5:

YOUR BIGGEST SUPERPOWER: CREATION

When I asked you to close your eyes at the beginning of the book, first you just looked at the back of your eyelids. But then I asked you to imagine being at the beach. You probably imagined the beach you visited most recently because that's what our brain does when we ask for information–it shows us a familiar image to help make sense of what we are seeing. The moment I said "beach," you involuntarily activated your pineal gland, and you imagined or saw a beach. Your pineal gland is a small melatonin-making gland, shaped like a pinecone, behind the bridge of your nose. It's been called our "third eye" because it is the part of the body we access when we imagine anything that isn't in front of our actual, physical eyes. When I make a grocery list for my husband, I imagine the grocery store we frequent, pretending I'm there myself. I pass the bakery and on to the cheese. Do we need feta? The concept of our third eye is easily understood by children. "You have a secret, hidden third eye," I tell them. "You have to close your first two eyes to find it, and it's your biggest superpower."

The pineal deals with the modulation of wake and sleep patterns, and some say it is the seat of our soul. It is also where our physical and spiritual aspects unite. This is interesting because it's during sleep that our astral bodies (woo-woo for the part of us that can leave our physical bodies) accomplish spiritual endeavors in all the other realms our physical bodies don't consciously know to exist. The recovering-overachiever in me likes to think of it like we can accomplish something while we sleep, and we can. Before sleeping at night, I often ask for conflicts to be resolved between me and the highest version of anyone with whom I'm upset. I create a space for this resolution to occur by asking for it to happen. How do we want our sleep spent? Obviously, our physical bodies are rejuvenating in our beds so we want peace, but meanwhile our consciousness, our light, does not sit around waiting for the sun to rise. As an author, I ask before sleep to receive the information children and their families need at this time. I asked to receive the words I wrote in this book while I slept. And I also send positive thoughts into the following day, imagining with my third eye all the important and fun things I have planned and exactly how I want them to unfold.

So, our third eye is like a time machine or portal our consciousness slips through to sleep-travel, go back to our childhood kitchen, find our missing keys, cloak protection over our children during the night, day-dream about shopping at Nordstrom's, or obsess over a coworker who has never liked you. If you closed your eyes and imagined you were in your car, you'd be using your third eye to get yourself there. I like to imagine my third eye as a projector I turn on and then watch to see what's projected on the screen. I think beach, and I see the beach I took my kids to last. I go to that exact spot in Destin, Florida, for just a moment. One of my go-to tools is to lie down for even three minutes wherever I can find space and breathe while going to the beach, which is my favorite place, in my mind. Mostly I use this tool to connect to the source beneath our feet (more about that in chapter seven), but I couldn't reap the tool's benefits if I didn't know I had access to more than just what is in front of my face. We can quite literally go anywhere using our third eye, faith, and a little stillness.

If upset, I have to force a breath, and then I see the beach. I breathe again and I remember the warmth of the sand. I'm there, and I breathe again, feeling the warm sun on my skin. I'm creating this healing space for myself when my physical reality is causing me stress.

My safe space is there for me anytime. When stressed, I pause and remind myself, I am light. I am only here in this body temporarily to learn something important with these souls I love, who challenge me in ways that will ultimately lead to my highest and best evolution. I can't always accomplish all this at once, but when I start with a breath and then just focus on my light, I can guide myself away from my anxiety a little at a time. I breathe into my light and ask it to soothe me and to remove anything that doesn't belong to me from my personal energy field (or what I like to imagine as a glass fishbowl around me, which works great with kids). It doesn't matter what it is clouding my water or whose fingerprints are on the glass outside. I am the creator of my reality, and when I'm conscious enough to catch myself before I spiral with emotion, I can command my equilibrium to be returned.

When you think about the unfriendly coworker or the feuding neighbor, you're literally hanging out in their energy field filled with their emotions. You're plugging yourself into their slimy glass fishbowl and swimming in their yucky water. They have defenses built up from living in their own conditions for years, but whatever trauma and drama they've experienced is new and excruciating to you. This is why we feel worse and worse the longer we worry, obsess, and see what we don't want to happen. We send a zap of negative energy to the crappy situation or person, they feel it subconsciously, think of you, and then join you in heaping more crap onto the conflict. Suddenly your not-so-favorite people are thinking about you all day, too, because you've tapped them, just like I'd tap my best friend in middle school by thinking about calling her and she would suddenly call me.

Affirmation for Reversing Negative Flow to a Situation or Relationship

For example, if I find myself thinking about someone or something that upsets me or takes my breath away, I stop and say, "I ask for the highest and best for the relationship between myself and [person's name]," or "Please bless [situation] with the highest and best available."

Affirmations like these are great places to start when you need to place positive energy and intention onto a relationship or situation about which you feel negatively. The words act as a place holder and reverse the negative flow that has kept you stuck in the emotion.

Switch the Flow to Positive

Imagine what it does to our children when we lie in bed at night worrying about them. It's like we're sending images of disaster over to their energy field while they sleep. Imagine two jars by their bedside that will collect all thoughts projected toward them. One reads, "All the amazing stuff" and the other, "Disaster." Which one do we want to fill first? Why not, if you are going to create anything for your children, send the best you can imagine. Ask for the highest and best thing the universe can offer. Put blankets of love, peace, truth, and compassion–anything you can imagine–over them in your imagination using your third eye. They can feel it, and cumulatively this creates change. Maybe they sleep better or have fewer night terrors. How do you know it's working? Well, how is worrying working? Any change in behavior that moves the flow of negative thoughts into positive is worth practicing. I recommend to my clients beginning a simple evening routine with your child of setting bedtime intentions. For me, this looks like a prayer together while I sit on the edge of their bed. With my words directed to God, my children hear my intentions of covering them with love and peace, and they hear me send positive energy to various situations and people. This is the opposite of worrying. This is modeling connection to something bigger and a belief in our personal power and connection with God/Source.

If you lay awake sending your relationship with your neighbor thoughts of compassion and love, you'd be mending the cord between you energetically while you sleep. It's, indeed, the opposite of worrying. The neighbor would unconsciously think of you, since you tapped him, but he'd wake up the next morning suddenly ready to be a bit more reasonable. Maybe the shift is only one degree toward kindness, but again any move toward positive and light is worth doing. Suddenly he considers your perspective. Maybe he decides to rent a storage spot for his RV. This is all very similar to the plants listening to angry or loving music. If the Metallica music was suddenly replaced with classical, those plants would gradually shift away from harsh and back to peaceful connection. You have to play different music for your neighbor in order to get the result you really want. Try Mozart. What you really want is to be neighborly and friendly with this man. You want him to like you. You want him to understand your point of view and be reasonable. Remember when I said earlier that your human, or physical body, gets hungry, angry, grumpy, and tired. So when you feel these things, get back into your light and remember your connection with Source. Schedule self-care or a short visit to the beach in your mind. And remember it's also your human side–your ego in fact–that tells you a little story about your neighbor that makes you angry and want to defend yourself. You tell your husband the neighbor won't get away with it, and you make plans to have a sheriff come out to handle the RV. Ask yourself, what is the truth about this conflict? Imagine having a higher perspective on it, as if you're a parent and your human and the neighbor are the feuding children. Step back and see the story for what it is.

Not to get biblical on you, but remember that you and this neighbor are two loops in the same fishing net. If you stay in your human, your ego–the part of you that says "it's not fair" and "I must be right"–your relationship or lack of one will weigh down the rest of the net. If you think about a golden fishing net wrapped around the planet, we need every loop to be solid and every knot pulled snug. In the same way we'd starve with a fishnet full of holes, we'll never break this unconscious spell that is cast over most of our planet, making us think we are not connected, if we don't work with our supposed enemies to mend our corner of the net. Analogies aside, we must aim to be our biggest, wisest versions of ourselves so we can determine the truth about each conflict we face and solve it with compassion and love.

When Things Feel Hard, Command a Shift

Try these four ways to create a more peaceful space in your body and mind the next time your child feels overcome with conflict or emotion. Start with calming yourself so you can then offer your child help, in the same way you have to place the oxygen mask on yourself first in case of emergency on a plane. You can explain these concepts to your child in whatever creative way you think will benefit him:

Breathe: Stopping to breathe while thinking negatively about someone or something allows us to become conscious of the universe around us and what solutions it's offering us now. Oxygen is our bodies' biggest healer. Get hooked. Imagine an oxygen bag dropping like on an airplane and breathe. With children, we breathe in slowly for the count of 1-2-3, hold for 1-2-3, and exhale slowly for 1-2-3.

Namaste: Next remember your light and the light in the other who is triggering big emotion in you. We are one. The blessing Namaste (despite setting off woo-woo alarms) beautifully means "I bow to the God, or divine, in you." Don't leave darkness where you can shine some light. Your child's teacher crossed a line with your son? Turn the situation over in your mind until you can shine some light into its cracks. We all do the best we can with the information and tools we have.

Witness: Become the witness of the challenge, instead of being stuck as a participant. Marisa Moris, author of several books, including *Attunement*, compares conflict to being stuck in quicksand. You must climb out of the quicksand in order to help anyone else who is also stuck. "Be in the world, but not of the world," or keep your perspective, and my favorite, "remember who you are" and why you're here.

Heal: If you can identify your specific challenging (or "big") emotion and pause, close your eyes and ask your inner knowing where in your body emotion is stuck. Where ever your body takes your attention, ask your light to go there and begin to heal it. You can ask it to receive light straight from God (or what I call "Source light") for the next twelve hours. Trust yourself. There are no wrong answers. Just take your consciousness to your hurt knee or the place your body says it's stuck, for example, and ask for your light to join with Source in healing you. This happens because you intend for it to. Remember the painful or uncomfortable feelings are not always your own. Your fishbowl has taken on someone else's conditions, and whatever they're triggering in you needs to be healed. Feel it to heal it, and be thankful for the opportunity.

No amount of well wishes or positive thinking will immediately change another person, but if each inter-action and each thought puts a pebble in a jar marked "love" or "hate" for that relationship, which jar do you want to fill first? You're in control. This is huge news. We are so powerful! And this is information I needed as a kid. This is information your kid needs. I didn't know I mattered at all, much less that I could affect my life with the way I thought and with the intentions I set as I woke each morning. As we get our households ready each morning, we can affect outcomes. Like an artist, every morning from our bed, we can design our day. Our thoughts are like paintbrushes, painting light or dark as we chose, and if we stay conscious, we can use only the brightest and best colors.

When I wake on the day of a flight, for example, I do a dry run in my head of my travel day. I am creating exactly what I want to happen by seeing it, or practicing it, with my third eye. There are studies showing people perform better in sports like swimming when they practice a race with their mind's eye before the actual race. You send a piece of your consciousness there via your third eye, you see it going well, and you leave your intentions and energy there, preparing the space for your success. When we tell or ask the universe what we want and see it happening, our vision will manifest easier as if our ideal experience–the highest and best experience possible–has muscle memory from doing it already. I imagine in my mind preparing my bags with ease and grace, climbing into an Uber with a driver I'm aligned with, arriving at the airport with perfect timing, gliding through TSA, finding food or magazines or whatever is important to me, and then I see my seat on the plane. I ask for the highest and best of the pilots and crew and every passenger on board, and I ask for a bubble of protection and light to be placed around the plane, carrying it effortlessly to my final destination. You get the point. This hardly takes any effort at all after a little practice, and I can relax knowing the universe and I have paved the way for success.

> **Affirmation**
> "Universe, connect me with people and circumstances that are for my (or my child's) highest and best good today."

Affirmation is one way we create. The words "I am" are very powerful, the most powerful in fact because, remember, we are creators in the same exact way our one true Source is a creator. Sure, the scale is smaller since we are currently creating on a planet Source created, but the highest aspect of every single living thing is Source. So the words we place after "I am" are what we become because we are commanding it. You cast a vote for more of what follows each and every "I am." "I am broke" puts a message of "broke" into your fishbowl, and it floats there with all the other self-creations you've declared into being. Try the following affirmation instead.

> **Affirmation**
> "I ask for the highest and best of the universe for my family. I am ready to be rewarded and I receive."
> "I live in an abundant and generous universe that supplies me with all I need."

Tell the Universe What You Want

I was taught to be miserable in order to punish the people who made me miserable, which is a painful logic.

It was so ingrained that it is to this day easier for me to complain, blame others, practice negative self-talk, mope, and basically hide from the world. But that is not the woman, mother, and coach I want to be. That is not the behavior of the author and minister I now am. So when my human body tells me everything sucks, or my words start sounding like blame, I turn to affirmation and often say "cancel" out loud, which is like telling the universe you withdraw your last comment or action. It withdraws it from your subconscious.

When it came to reaching the families of the children who needed my help, I spoke my soul's desire out loud. "Let me be a minister of light to help young people who suffer as I did. Send light ahead of me, and show me my next steps." I was loud and proud so the universe was clear. I stated what my soul was longing for louder than my loudest self-doubting thought. Affirmation is the best way to fake it 'til you make it. I've sat alone with my sobs many times until I mustered up the courage to call back a negative thought and cancel a declaration of failure. I find a pause to get conscious of my light again, and I use my tools for connection. During the writing of this book, whether while piecing together the purpose of my sad childhood, or having doubt creep in about the validity of this subject, I met my tears with "I am a clear channel to my light and my Source, and there are children who need this book."

If It Is to Be, It Must Be Me

If I wake up at 4:00 a.m. and my body aches from the toddler years of little deep sleep, I let the fatigue have my body, but not my mind. "I am filled with abundant life force energy with each deep breath I take," and I commit to deep breaths while I dress and tiptoe in the dark. Could I be frustrated and let that steal my precious breath? Yes. But I tried that for years, and that behavior is not a characteristic of the person I want to be. "I am now the me who slept eight hours uninterrupted." Inhale. Exhale. Do I sometimes not want to think this way? Yes. Do I still cry and whine sometimes? Definitely. But most of the time I do not take this heaviness into my morning or project it onto my family. I find a small pause and find my light. What kind of person do I want to be? My light is bigger than any obstacle. I can create a beautiful day despite my lack of sleep. I decide to make it a good day for myself. And I remind myself my children are watching. I will model for them better coping mechanisms than I was taught. I will contribute to their precious emotional and spiritual wellness, and as I do this I contribute to my own healing.

Let's be real: we cannot go long on little sleep, and we can't give from an empty cup. I learned this the hard way, but after clogged milk ducts, a MRSA infection, pneumonia, and adrenal fatigue, I learned to nap. I feed my body nourishing real food and rub my own feet despite what the voice in my head says about my self-worth. That voice is a liar. I cannot remove it completely because it was put there when I was young and absorbing and believing everything, but I can choose to not listen. When I think I should skip a meal or a nap and just push on, I choose to love myself instead and take care of my kids' momma just like I take care of them. And in that moment, I'm healing myself. Self-care is something I create space for so I can better parent my children and also so they'll take kind and gentle care of themselves one day when I'm not around.

Visualization

Whenever something isn't going your way or a person is trying to enter into an argument, excuse yourself briefly, and close your eyes. Breathe deeply and imagine yourself with the situation in perfect resolution. Envision a few details and success. Ask for compassion and love to be showered over all involved.

Chapter 6:

YOUR PLAYING FIELD

Have you ever walked into a place and not liked how it felt and thought, "I've gotta get out of here?" Have you ever gone into a bar during the day to use a bathroom or ask for directions and get hit with the place's stale and cold feel? No matter how you've explained this to yourself before, this is you feeling energy. This is your inner being deciphering the energy field of a place. There is no doubt there is a difference between how it feels inside a stale bar compared to how it feels inside a cathedral or inside a happy home. Now how about people? Some people feel better to you than others. Sometimes you walk into a room full of people and fixate on someone either because you're drawn to him or her or because you feel like you should be wary. Part of this is intuition, but mostly this is you being repelled by energy you cannot see in the same way you'd grab your nose if you walked into a kitchen full of rotting food. You might not be able to see the mold or maggots right away, but your body tells you they're there. This is because every object, living and inanimate, has energy, and whether we believe it or not, we are able to discern this energy to protect ourselves and our families.

The reason the bar and church have such contrasting energies is because of the contrasting intentions of the people visiting the spaces. People who are in a bar are drinking. While you can certainly have a drink and not have bad energy, for the most part people in bars are being unconscious. They are not thinking at all about their lights, their connection to one another, or their connection to Source, and those empty intentions linger. I know that when I was unconscious all those years, I was also afraid because I didn't have an explanation for why I was here or a direction for what I should be doing that made me want to live. Since most people walk around asleep in life, unconscious of our divine purpose and connection and light inside, it's a good guess that most people are suffering from painful uncertainty and fear around existential topics. I think it's safe to say most people feel lost, if they're honest. So we send our sensitive, yet powerful, children out into the world when they're little, with their crystal clear water and sparkling glass, and their interactions with unconscious, damaged people affect them deeply. But what if I told you we can teach children to feel for foreign, yucky energies entering their field? We all have the power to monitor and command our energies, and now we'll learn how to toss out what we don't want, just like we'd pick up a piece of trash or dog poop from our front yards. "Who left this here?!" we'd say out on the sidewalk, and we'd get our yard back to the way we wanted it right away.

Is Your Child an Empath?

In church, the intentions of its visitors are quite the opposite of those in a bar. It's rare for someone to enter a church without some intention of connecting with Source (even if it's sourced by guilt), but regardless, people's intentions for attending church are usually positive. Each person, place, or thing's energy is based on what intentions it has itself or what intentions people who use it have. This is why objects have special meaning to people, especially to children. If a child loses their cherished stuffed animal, you can't just hand them another one. When a loved one leaves their body and dies, we can actually feel the person on their objects and clothes.

If we could look at the energy field (or what the woo-woos call an aura) of a child's favorite stuffed animal, we would find all the child's intentions of love and comfort. But if the child was often scared, crying, or alone while holding the animal, its field could also hold fear, sadness, confusion, or abandonment. So we can imagine that everyone we meet is holding their issues and experiences–good and bad– in their energy field, or fishbowl. The most sensitive among us, often children, can feel the energy of everyone all the time. These people are called empaths. I am an empath, which is why life was so painful for over thirty years. But once I knew I could pick up on others' energy fields, I got to work finding solutions. And the solution is to take charge of your energy, clear it often, and be prepared to protect yourself before and after encountering stressful energies.

We hold our experiences and feelings in the water of our fishbowls. So, the best imagery for clearing and cleaning our personal energy fields is a fishbowl. Fishbowls are made of clear glass, are round, have an opening in the top, and most kids can imagine one easily.

Cleaning Your Fishbowl Exercise

1. Close your eyes and ground yourself by saying out loud or in your head, "I am [your name] and only [your name]," and call all of your attention and energy back into your body.

2. Next, say "I am now inside a fishbowl," and imagine your physical body standing in the middle of a fishbowl with glass and water around you. Do you observe any sensations?

Maybe it feels cold, dark, or crowded. If this is difficult, challenge yourself to come up with one adjective.

3. With your eyes still closed, ask that Source light come straight down from above, through the hole in the fishbowl's top, and clean your physical body, which stands like a little statue in the middle of the bowl. Whatever this looks like to you is correct. Witness your body being cleaned. Trust it's happening, and pay attention to any sensations or impressions you realize. Remember your intention is for all foreign matter to leave.

4. Next, ask Source light to come straight down and clean the water. You can imagine a little green net with a handle like the ones used to clean fishbowls. You can watch a colander-type object strain the water from below, or let your brain clean it however it wants.

5. Last, ask Source light to come straight down and clean the inside of the glass and then the outside. Perhaps a white polishing glove comes into the bowl and shines the glass until it squeaks. Or maybe the hand sprays a blue liquid on the glass and wipes it clear. Sometimes I imagine a little squeegee.

6. Now that your fishbowl is clean, you have removed everything that doesn't belong to you.

People will receive you as 100 percent yourself because you are! You will not trigger others with your foreign energy; you'll be alone in your fish-bowl, and you'll feel great.

A newborn baby's fishbowl mostly has clean, fil-tered water and sparkling clear glass. If that baby's par-ents wanted him to be the opposite sex, however, plop goes a chunk of disappointment into the baby's field. The water becomes murkier in first grade when he starts riding the school bus. The driver's been in an emotion-ally abusive relationship for several decades and carries rage and suicidal thoughts around in her bowl. Your child says he doesn't like the bus driver, even though she rarely speaks, and he wishes you would drive him. Another little boy at school has a parent who drinks and sometimes hits his mom. Your son often gets into squabbles with this child and hit him twice before being removed from the class. There is no abuse in your home, so why does he react this way? Your son can feel this other kid's abuse. Your son can feel the bus driver's rage and is scared, and it doesn't make sense to your child either. After a conflict, he's left thinking he's bad, and you're left thinking you must be a bad parent. Nei-ther is true! Hear me say this: your child is a being of light and love, and since no one is telling him this, he's forgetting it. Being an empath, he cannot distinguish between his own emotions and those of people around him. The sooner he learns this in an age-appropriate way, and the sooner he learns to clean his fishbowl, the sooner he'll start distinguishing between his own and foreign energies.

Empaths feel energy in a major way, far more so than the rest of the population. There are plenty of adult empaths, and sadly many are alcoholics or addicts because they've dealt with hard, scary emotions their whole lives without explanation. They endured feeling the traumas of the adults who raised them, feeling like they were at fault and entangled with heavy emotions they shouldn't have had to deal with. They learned to self-medicate and numb their emotions. They've been blamed and given up on because their families think they are the problem. Many adult empaths today are in prison and have no idea they are gifted or that there are solutions to their pain. They can access more of their brain, which makes them able to feel emotions from someone one hundred feet away. With information and support, they could turn this gift into a positive, life-changing endeavor that could help others.

Fishbowl When Already Experiencing Stress

Often, we are struck down in the midst of our day with a big stress event. Sometimes it's something small that bothered you more than you thought it should. Sometimes we're just agitated and aren't sure why. Clearing my fishbowl is my go-to when I'm feeling conflict. First, do a regular fishbowl visualization. Next, sitting with your eyes still closed, ask, "Where in my fishbowl am I carrying [insert problem like 'conflict with my partner']?" Send light to the area you're directed to and command anything that isn't for your highest and best good to leave now. Breathe oxygen into the area, and as you exhale imagine dark energy leaving your body through your mouth.

Fishbowl to Protect Self for Day

After clearing your statue, water, and glass, say, "Source, today please fill up my fishbowl and surround me with compassion, love, and peace. May I project these things and be met with the same."

Fishbowl to Heal Blocks

If you are dealing with trauma in a relationship or indecision in career, for example, you can ask for help using your fishbowl. After clearing your statue, water, and glass, say, "Source, I ask for help with [insert issue like 'my relationship with my daughter']. Please guide me as I remove any obstacles to love with her in my field forever." Watch what is presented to you. Watch the obstacle leave your field.

***

My Gift to You

To receive an audio recording of the fishbowl exercise with Kat, send an email to hello@katmulvaney.com and let us know you're ready for your "little bit of woo."

***

For lessons or sessions to help with the energy in your home and family, visit www.enteringtheheart. com. Entering the Heart provides energetic clearings of homes, individuals, and ancestral lines; and also gives lessons in sound healing and Feng Shui, both of which help many sensitive children (sessions on Zoom or Skype available).

Chapter 7:

YOUR LIMITLESS SOURCE

'**ve discussed how the source of our light is the same
being most religions talk about and call God, except
Source isn't one person or a mystery in the sky. Source
is electricity and represents the collective power of all our
light combined. There is nothing that cannot be accomplished through it. As if the most majestic and sparkling
glass chandelier shattered into trillions and trillions of
pieces—this is how Source experiences its creations–the
galaxies, planets, and beings like humans. When your
light isn't in a body, it's together with Source, wrapped
up into a hug like you could only get when not in your
body. When I held my babies, it was like I couldn't get
close enough to them. I could snuggle them and press
our bodies together. I could nurse them and smell their
heads, but I found myself wanting to be closer. I was

wanting to break through the barrier of these bodies and touch my light to theirs. I had not been this close with them for over thirty years (since my light entered this body), and I was yearning to be one with them, embraced in a hug with no barriers between our light. It's like we are all scuba diving and can only get as close as the sealed fabric and oxygen tanks will allow.

My children's light saved me. They were how Source lowered me a lifeline. They were the first lights I recognized that woke me up and the first lights that sought mine out and offered me unconditional love. Even though I had to help them with every physical need, and still do, they reminded me of my light and my worth, making it seem like they were the ones carrying and caring for me. Babies are often Source's plan to rescue our lost souls, and it was definitely so with my daughter. Her energy came around before she was conceived, and I know it was her influence that got me to finally complete a spiritual yoga teacher training I'd been dreaming of for ten years. That led to more and more metaphysical training, and while I was pregnant with her, I meditated every day, bringing colors of light down from Source and into my seven chakras, which are energy centers in our bodies, starting at the base of our tailbone and ending at our crown. And it was while I was bringing colors into my aura, with my hands on my belly, that I started thinking how much kids, especially struggling ones, needed resources like the visualization I was practicing. In learning about grounding and other alternative approaches, I opened myself up even more to my life's work. My daughter's soul needed me to get peaceful and grounded in order to welcome her into the world this time, and in preparing for her, I reignited my purpose. I wanted her to have tools I never had. I knew I could help spare other kids from the pain I experienced as a teen and young adult. My daughter's light managed to crack me open just enough that I woke up and remembered why I was here.

I know that my children and I, just like my parents and I before, made a contract to help each other learn certain things. I know that our perfect Source, which I am a part of, had a plan. I trust it. I know Source is sending down what we need at all times, but we have to set the intention to receive it. I didn't feel evidence of our ability to receive directly from Source until I sat purposely with my daughter in my belly and my eyes closed, inviting in what I needed at that time in the form of colors. We just have to know it's coming to receive it, which makes this direct connection to Source so exciting. It's as simple as saying right now for the first time in your life, "I receive. I receive every bit of love and compassion I've ever missed out on right now. I accept what my highest self and Source are sending me today." We can create the environment we need to support our mission by trusting Source and telling it what we want. We can cast out all fear and trust that we are limitless because we are part of our limitless Source. This is called faith.

When I pray, or talk to Source, it's like I'm talking to the entirety of life force energy in the whole universe – to the whole collective consciousness, not just on our Earth but to however big Source spreads out. So I'm accessing all the knowledge and wisdom and love that exists anywhere. This is why meditation works. I sit in silence with the intention of finding solutions and peace, and afterward, I have fresh perspective and feel peaceful. Praying is talking to Source, and meditating is listening to Source. If we have a problem, we have two choices: we can find distractions that drown out communication with Source, which is what most people do, or we can find silence or stillness in order to receive answers. I find silence in walks in the woods or hot baths when no one is home, and I find stillness in a daily yoga practice and in sitting comfortably with my eyes closed for as little as five minutes at a time. And the more I find stillness and silence, the more I can switch my perspective to that of the observer, the witness, when I get entangled in all the things unconscious humans do. For example, when I can become the witness when my child is upset or whining loudly, I'm able to show compassion – the compassion of our Source – because I've connected to a larger version of myself and asked my irritated human self to take the backseat. Compassion is when we see ourselves in another, especially in another who is struggling, and it's an attribute parents need when learning how to redirect the flow of emotions.

"You are not a drop in the ocean. You are the entire ocean in a drop."
– Rumi

A Review: Two Ways Source Supports from Above

1. Once we are conscious of being one with Source, we can make a shift to looking at our problems from the outside as the observer with compassion. Compassion is seeing ourselves in another person, who is struggling, with love and without judgment. We can also know Source looks on us with compassion when we struggle and ask for it anytime.

2. When we feel stress in our body or big emotions creeping in, we can close our eyes and ask for help from Source above, bringing light down into our fishbowls to clear out the intruder and bring in new, peaceful energies.

The Source Beneath Our Feet

Now that you know how the source of our light above helps and supports us, let's look at our source below–our mother Earth. The Earth is a living being, a complex and miraculous creature, created by Source to birth bodies to hold his slices of light. Earth makes it possible for our slices of light to keep coming down to learn and evolve. And in the billions of years since the Earth was created, it has evolved just as much as the creatures that walk on its ground and swim in its oceans. Source will keep experiencing life through humans, as long as humans don't destroy our bodies or our planet. Human bodies come from the earth, in the same way our light is sourced from above. When we die, our light goes back to Source above, and our body goes back into the earth. Sadly, most people do not see the significance of our bodies as something that houses our brilliant light, our soul. Most people are spiritually unconscious, as we've discussed, passing the characteristic on to their children, but equally as sad is most people are also physically unconscious. If we can realize our physical body's connection and reliance on the earth, we can use it and its many gifts as tools for healing and clarity.

Just like people have lost touch with their lights and are relying on their human ego and on sources outside of them like media (magazines, MSNBC, FOX, CNN, MTV, etc.) and for-profit industries (food, beverage, pharmaceutical, etc.) to lead them, people have mostly forgotten that the Earth supports its creations without fail. Unfortunately, the Earth doesn't have advertising budgets and has no high-paid executives pushing its agenda, so it's been decades since humans trusted it for their food and medicine. Our disconnection from our bodies' source is of course a symptom of our disconnection from the source of our light, and if we can reconnect to both our sources, we'll get to experience what we were intended to: connection, love, and perfect health.

Remember in biology when they taught us the kingdoms of life? It's easy to forget how much life exists beneath the humans, even smaller than the animals and plants we eat. There are categories that include elements and minerals we could not live without, and many are healing and available at our fingertips. The Earth is truly here to support us in many ways.

The Best Medicines Are Free

Earthing is walking barefoot on earth – grass, sand, dirt, rock, or shallow water. Ditch your shoes once a day, stand on your source below, and close your eyes. Ask whatever doesn't serve you to leave through the bottoms of your feet and be dissolved into the mineral kingdom. Or you can ask to be recharged by the center of the Earth and pull up life force energy through long straws in your feet. With your eyes closed, you can identify the energy moving up your body and filling you with a beautiful color or whatever you ask for at the time. Children love earthing because they would often rather be barefoot but also because they can feel the Earth's steady and strong energy, especially if they have previously spent little time outdoors barefoot.

Oxygen is one huge reason our lights come into bodies. There is a reason they pump it into casinos in Vegas. It's invigorating, dynamite brain food, and deeply healing to our bodies. The more oxygen you bring into your body, the more dark and stale energies will be forced out. To calm myself I inhale deeply through my nose and out my mouth, trying to extend each as long as possible. I inhale "God" and exhale "peace." With my young children, we do the 1-2-3 breathing (explained in chapter five). To clear and energize myself, I practice a three-part breath entirely out of my mouth. It consists of two deep, gulping mouth inhales and one quick and deep mouth exhale, and it's usually done for fifteen to twenty minutes without stopping. Breathwork has done more for my anxiety and healing than any other modality. Teachers like David Elliot (https://www.davidelliott.com) and Michael Brian Baker (https://thebreathcenter.com) sell guided meditations, walking you through this particular kind of breathwork, and they also offer in-person workshops.

Water is my favorite element. My children and I take at least one bath per day, and I add Epsom salt from the earth for detoxifying and an essential oil like lavender for relaxation. We run out into the rain and jump in puddles, we listen to moving water noises at bedtime, and we visit rivers and oceans and swimming pools. Water is healing and with a little salt and intention, you can soak away all your physical and emotional cares.

Real food from the earth can heal our bodies and clear our minds. Often children who are sensitive to energy are also sensitive to the energy of food. If anyone in my home is experiencing a health issue, we eliminate anything that is not close to Source. Cut added sugar for honey, processed juice for water and black decaf teas, packaged snacks for fruit. My kids say we eat food that comes from God, and they're right. Before greed took over the food industry somewhere around the 1950s, people grew food in their yards or communities for their families. They ate colorful, varied foods that were in season and fermented the portions they couldn't eat. They hunted animals and used the whole carcass, including the organ meats and tendons. They didn't profit off their food and instead traded it with others, which gave them access to even more variety. The food was grown in rich soil, so the nutrient-density was high, and their families were well-fed and healthy. Since profit wasn't the objective, food wasn't treated with chemicals like glyphosate to kill bugs and allow for bigger crops and bigger profit. But once large corporations made feeding people their business, small-scale, honest farming became an endangered practice.

Now, food without chemicals and grown without scientific shortcuts has to be labeled "organic" and is unaffordable for most families. Most of our affordable produce is saturated with toxic chemicals and made with genetically modified organisms (GMOs), none of which our cells know what to do with, and it's an issue that is driving our tragic health crisis, which includes children in alarming rates. In the past few years, small farmers and local farmers' markets have become more popular, but this untreated and honorably grown food is expensive. One of my favorite resources for finding local farmers is an organization called the Weston A. Price Foundation, or WAPF (www.westonaprice.org). Also run by the WAPF, www.RealMilk.com is a directory of farmers who sell fresh milk and oftentimes meat and vegetables as well. Enter your zip code to find a list of farmers in your area.

The key to using the earth's food as a pathway to wellness for your family is avoiding food made by companies who don't care about your health. Ingredients matter. Anything with a barcode is at risk of having ingredients that risk your and your children's health. Most companies use the cheapest ingredients they can get away with in order to drive profits. One of the biggest areas of concern are the fats most packaged foods use. Highly processed vegetable oils like canola are mostly industrial waste products the food industry fooled consumers into purchasing in huge amounts starting in the

1980s. Vegetables aren't fatty in the first place, which should make the thoughtful shopper suspicious. In general, buy organic foods with ingredients you recognize and ask yourself if the company who made it has your child's health in mind.

Ways to Keep Your Family's Food Close to the Earth

- Try to eat foods directly from the earth, avoiding processing and packaging.
- Avoid vegetable oils and instead use grass-fed butter, ghee, lard, tallow, and coconut oil – all earth fats.
- Buy grass-fed meats because you want to consume animals who eat their biological norm, not a cheap feed that puts more dollars in the food companies' pockets and wrecks our health.
- Buy wild-caught seafood, and be aware of what fish has higher levels of mercury and avoid them.
- Seek out organic foods on sale, buy in bulk, and make sure you're familiar with the "dirty dozen," a list of produce that is the most important to eat organic.

strawberries	nectarines	peaches	tomatoes
spinach	apples	cherries	celery
sweet bell peppers	grapes	pears	potatoes

- If buying packaged foods, choose ones with as few ingredients as possible. If you cannot pronounce an ingredient, skip it. Processed foods have the same effect on our bodies as stale, negative energy.

- Grains, while grown on the earth, have been wildly abused and ruined by the food industry in the last half-century. Most people who are gluten sensitive are really reacting to the large amount of glyphosate that's poured on most American grain. All grain will be better processed by your body if it is yeast free, sprouted (or fermented), and organic.

- Eat colorful foods like vegetables first during meals, so you fill up mostly on high-energy foods straight from Source. Earth's foods have amazing healing powers.

- Be patient. It takes taste buds several weeks to stop expecting sweetened and processed foods. If real food is all there is in your home, your family will eat it eventually, and the results will come. The Whole 30 diet is a great way to get started eating real food and can be found easily online.

- Examples of "God food" snacks:
  - Celery sticks with cream cheese or peanut butter
  - Smoked salmon and sliced cucumbers

- ▪ Cashews and raisins; walnuts and grapes
- ▪ Mini oranges and beef jerky
- ▪ Hard-boiled eggs and sliced apple
- Sneak in nutrients. Don't underestimate adding accessory God foods like squeezing a lemon into your water, adding chopped parsley or cilantro to your foods, make a green juice in the morning, add two more colors to your salad with a radish or pepper, chop garlic or ginger for your salad dressing, add berries to your oatmeal, and hide vegetables in your muffins and quiches.

The Genius of a Mother's Body

The miracle of our physical body starts in a woman's body. The process of growing and birthing a baby is beyond amazing. The splendor and precision of this creation process should be enough to convince people there is a God, yet most of the miracle of birth has been stolen by a medical industry that is not aware of babies' light, by an industry that is fear-based and does not recognize miracles or the body's ability to heal itself. After I birthed two babies, I finally saw my body as a gift and miracle straight from my earthly source. It gave me the ability to bring down my babies' lights and allow us to be together in this human form while we learn and grow. When I changed the way I viewed my physical body and began seeing it as powerful and as a channel of light, I was able to love it more and teach my children to love and care for theirs.

Once the baby is born, mothers' bodies produce breast milk for years if the supply is maintained. It is the perfect food and is so miraculous it kills cancer cells. Yet the practice of breastfeeding has been under attack by big food companies selling infant formula since the 1950s. At first, women were urged to breast-feed for six months and then switch to formula, but by the end of the '50s, many babies went straight to formula, bypassing one of the biggest miracles of birth and teaching women that their bodies weren't crucial to the health of their babies. Corporate greed and dis-honest, manipulative advertising have caused millions of people to forego this miracle food for their children. Breast is indeed best because it's the biological norm and what our creator intended. While some women cannot breastfeed for various health issues, my goal here is to simply tell parents that we have been lied to. In all instances, what comes from our earthly source is leaps and bounds better for our bodies than anything manufactured by for-profit companies. I'm thankful formula exists for families who cannot access breast-milk, but I'm saddened by the enormity of the formula lie, which makes many mommas think formula made by a for-profit company could be comparable to what Source intended.

Treasures from the Earth

We now know the power of earthing, putting our bare feet in the earth for a few minutes each day. Imagine if we were barefoot on the earth all day, every day and how connected and grounded we'd feel being inundated with so many healing properties. Since we can't stand barefoot outside all day, I want to tell you about healing treasures from the earth called crystals. Crystals are millions of years old and are remnants of the earliest part of the earth's formation. Scientifically, crystals are the most balanced structure that exists in nature, which is why they feel so good close to our bodies.

People have been attracted to crystals since the beginning of time for spiritual advancement because the stones' energies interact with our personal electromagnetic fields and the effects are noticeable and exciting. As you'd guess, crystals are fun and powerful tools for children of all ages. There are hundreds of shapes and colors to choose from. There are online resources to help select them, and some cities have shops to pick them out in person. Books like *The Crystal Bible* by Judy Hall describes the attributes and healing properties of hundreds of crystals like larimar, which brings calmness and removes foreign energies. Chrysoprase reduces nightmares in children. Moonstone and uncut ruby reduce hyperactivity, and moldavite is useful for sensitive children who suffer from deep emotions. If you

can name a symptom or desired effect, there is a crystal to help. If choosing a crystal in person, just browse
and see which ones catch your eye. Trust that your light
will guide you to the ones you need. Hold them in your
hands and near your heart and ask if it's the one for you.
Kids are so good at sensing and knowing which crystal
is right for them!

Ways to Use Crystals

1. Let your children pick ones they're drawn to and
   experiment with how they make them feel.
2. Place one by your bed (or your child's) during
   sleep, and note anything unusual. Maybe someone sleeps better. Maybe a conflict is resolved
   through a vivid dream.
3. Help your child collect crystals (and other
   objects from nature) and display them lovingly
   in his bedroom. As he dresses for the day, he can
   select one or more to carry in his pocket and pull
   them out to hold or put on a desk for comfort or
   courage. Knowing the special qualities (or super
   powers!) of each crystal will empower your child
   to take on those qualities for himself.
4. Place crystals on body parts to reduce pain or to
   break up stuck energy. Some children will enjoy
   lying down and having dozens of crystals laid on
   their bodies as a healing game.

5. Lay your crystals outside on the evening of the monthly full moon. The full moon energies will clear and super-charge them! Plus, kids love this activity! (Sometimes we even sleep in a tent during the full moon to clear and super-charge our bodies!)

Crystal Resources

1. Online shop and crystal coaching: www.Crystallounge.org
2. Online shop: www.belovedminerals.com
3. For information on crystal shapes, colors and more: www.crystalvaults.com

Chapter 8:

YOUR ENTOURAGE

Remember how you can send a piece of your consciousness to the beach? I send a piece of myself ahead of me on travel days, and as I drive to the mall, I imagine making a big loop in the parking lot as if I was already there circling for a spot. Placing my energy and intention there ahead of time helps me find a parking spot. This is me sending a piece of my light ahead of me, and it's like having a dozen personal assistants who help reduce my anxiety and increase my faith. Many people (on team woo) call these pieces of ourselves our "guides." There are people who swear by them and send them on errands to protect children and task them with finding much more than just parking spots. Getting in touch with your guides is as easy as saying, "please go ahead and find a parking spot," as you exit the highway and just seeing the lot in your mind. The energy that goes ahead of us is ourselves, and once we believe we can accomplish things in places where we are not physically present, the possibilities are endless. All it takes to start trying this is your new belief that you can influence your surroundings. Before I fall asleep, I imagine my kids' bed and wrap them in my love. I see them and imagine doing it, so that means it's done. It's that simple. But most people think this is nuts because they've been convinced we have no magic or power.

Instead of practicing a swim meet in your head the night before, "practice" getting everything you want the following day. See it, believe it, receive it. As long as it's for your highest and best, your positive intention will put your requests in motion, which is how prayer works. Prayer puts a pebble in the bucket representing a positive outcome, and it does make a difference. Prayer and visualization sends a piece of you – a member of your entourage – over to cast a vote for the outcome of a relationship, situation, or well-being of a specific person. You can practice and see yourself finding a parking spot before you get to the lot. See the meeting you're nervous about going the best way you can imagine, and know you're preparing the space for this success. Teach your child this technique to prepare their days ahead of time. See the mean kid receiving so much love in the form of red roses symbolizing love or a waterfall of beautiful colors that the energy between your child and her or him will be transmuted and redirected.

Love Scouts

Since we have these pieces of ourselves that act like personal assistants, we might as well send them on errands of love to fill that jar first. We might as well ask them to deliver good intentions to each person and situation we will encounter on our day. What if we send messages of love to all things, starting with ourselves? I don't mean to say out loud to everyone and everything "I love you." I mean wake in the morning and put your hands on your heart and say, "Good morning precious body. I love you and am grateful for you." If instead of sending success and positivity to my day of travel I sent worry and dread, I'd be tossing pebbles into the darker of the two jars. I'd be choosing the "fear" jar instead of the "trust." I trust a part of myself is always working for my highest and best good. Our assistants, our guides, are with us at all times, but they don't jump to attention until we invite them to help.

Now let's talk about the science of guides. Our guides are pieces of our brain, and as we call on them, sending them on errands and imagining them successful, we are firing synapses in our brain and making little sparks, literally bringing more light to our brains. Think of calling on your guides as sending your brain to the gym. The brain is a muscle, so practicing working with our guides will make us better at it, just like you can't get better at running unless you practice running. My guides help me with anxiety because I send them ahead of me like soldiers of peace, and my kids hear me saying, "Send light ahead of us, God" and "OK, light, find us the best parking spot!" This makes me proud because my children are learning about their power and learning to place faith and trust in the universe. Together, we tell the universe what we want and trust that what we receive is what we need at that precise time.

When Feeling Low, Go High

Your entourage of guides isn't the only energy hanging around you. Your energy attracts more of the same. So if your child is struggling with big, painful emotions, pieces of energy that match that low energy will come around guaranteed. Negative energy attracts negative energy like a magnet. The best I feel is when I'm grounded and alone in my body, meaning there are no foreign energies in my fishbowl, and I'm as close to Source as I can be while in my dense body. It also means I'm seeing life through my higher energy centers (chakras), like the sixth, which is the third eye and allows me to be the witness without being immersed, and the seventh, which is the crown of the head and receives light and information from Source (and is the opening at the top of our glass fishbowl). When I'm high like this, I'm unaffected by lower and darker energies. When you have just had a good night's sleep, went to the gym, and spent time in the sun, you are not irritated when someone cuts you off in traffic. When you sleep poorly and have been hunched over your desk for eight hours, your energy may be low, you are not connected to the source or your own divinity, and you might yell or cry in the same traffic scenario. Once we are aware of energy, we can experiment with it, clear it before it becomes overwhelming, and protect ourselves before we enter our day.

The key is preparing ahead of time. Being grounded and in our bodies saves us from most mishaps because here we are conscious. We can set the intention to rise into our crowns before we leave the house. We remember we're on Earth for a divine and important reason. We remember the challenging person we're dealing with is also here for a purpose, and he or she is at a different place in evolving than we are. We don't hold it against a fourth grader that he or she doesn't know calculus. We see their mood or actions are not about us but about them and their pain or fear. If we can keep ourselves lifted and conscious, we can hover above drama and deal with it much better since we are not drowning in it. Returning to the quicksand analogy from chapter five, we must climb out before we can accurately assess the situation and help others.

Now that I know about energy and know it's been the source of all my emotional pain and suffering, I choose to manage it with intention and care. Just like many physical afflictions are managed with medication, I have to manage my sensitivity to energy with tools that work. But also like other afflictions, I still have bad and hard days when I want to give up. I don't though because my kids need me to learn healthy and loving ways to care for myself so they can learn from me. Through me teaching my children about their lights and power, I am breaking the cycle of unconsciousness and pain that was passed on to me. Children everywhere need these tools broken down into simple language because it is through returning to our light and then protecting the heck out of it that we save millions of kids' lives who otherwise would find life too painful to bear.

Beings of Love

There are beings we can call on for help in addition to the various parts of our own brain.

Grandma, whose light is no longer in the physical body, still exists. And while she may have experienced Earth as several different humans over the course of time, you can call on one aspect of her, the one you knew, at any time. Both of my parents lost their youngest brother at a young age. My mother's little brother tragically fell off a waterfall when he was in college in 1981, and my father's youngest brother died of brain cancer in the mid-'90s. I frequently ask that the highest versions of them protect my children, and I always have the highest and best intentions for all involved. I never met my husband's mother, but I call on the highest version of her to help us whenever we're feeling lots of stress with our children or need the universe to support us.

Angels are not humans with wings like art history and stories teach us. They are energy like every other being not in body and act as the messengers and liaisons between Source and us. There is an angel or energy for every attribute in the universe. I ask that angels of joy come into my field when I'm struggling to find joy on my own, and I'm actually inviting the emotion joy into my fishbowl. I set the intention to invite joy in, and it comes. It's like I see joy walking by and I wave my hands. "I'll have some of that! Pick me!" If I see an ambulance rush past with its sirens blaring, I ask angels from Source to accompany it and help deliver the highest and best to whoever needs help. I don't intend to control situations or people, but I can send angels of peace to my home and bedroom as I lie down if the day has been stressful. I can ask angels of courage to accompany me when I speak to large audiences, and I ask angels of comfort to stick around my son who just started preschool. I do this easily now because I see that it works.

If when I was feeling joyless, I did what I used to do, no one, especially me, would feel joy because I'd be creating chaos and spreading my low energy like the flu. And since I want to be a joyous person more than anything else, I am willing to do what it takes to bring joy into my personal space. I ask the angels of joy to deliver that energy to me. And they do. Like the Leonard Cohen line, "There is a crack in everything. That's how the light gets in"; well, all it takes for the universe to send its angels is for you to ask. For you to remember that you are light and you can change. For you to know you can start to heal a feeling while you are in the feeling with awareness and desire to feel things differently than before. So when I'm joyless and tired and start to forget the point of it all, I get conscious, I remember my divinity, and I ask – sometimes not even nicely – for help. I consciously make a different choice to care for myself when distressed. I choose the solution that will raise me up and not bring me down.

The biggest turning point of my entire life happened shortly after I collapsed on my knees and cried hysterically, begging for help from God. I knew in that moment I had made a real breakthrough. I received help. I had made the space–cracked myself open just enough to let the light back in. I knew in that moment that if anyone could help me, only my one true Source could and would. My golden compass, my light, was restored that day on the hard Berber carpet in Boca Raton, Florida. I didn't have my spiritual awakening for real for another three years, but I knew from that day on things were getting better, and I made a series of important decisions that landed me where I am today.

Take the Best, Leave the Rest

Let's imagine a scale from one to ten. One is the lowest energy and least amount of light, and ten is the highest energy and most light. Every morning you wake up and start your day with a score on the light/dark scale. Let's say you wake up tomorrow and are only a four. You aren't so low you can't get out of bed, but you are not happy and already feel how challenging the day may be. As you leave your house and start interacting with people, you attract and trap in your fishbowl any energy you come in contact with that is a four and below, which will keep you in a low state the whole day. In the same way that there are magnificent and bright angels and archangels, the opposite also exists. Archangels are the energy and light closest to God, and you do not want the opposite end of the spectrum hanging around you or your kids. When you're in a low state you attract low energies, like the low energy of someone who died recently who was angry and sick and did not have any connection to Source. Again, these beings, light and dark, are energy and do not look like people, yet they can feel more concrete when their energies come close, and kids are even more susceptible to these energies because their lights are so bright.

If you look at the energy you attract as your entourage who will follow you around and stick its nose in all your affairs, you want to make sure you're at the highest you can be to attract cool buddies. If I'm feeling a four or five when I pull out of my driveway in the morning, I'm struggling but I don't lose time to my emotions anymore. I am able to stay conscious through my hard emotions, I stay conscious of Source, and I pull out my grounding and clearing tools.

Ways to Raise Your Energy Score

1. Play music you love. Consider classical, choir, monks chanting, nature sounds, or specific frequencies to improve the energy in your home. Sound healing is one of the greatest tools for children. Search for the following "Solfeggio frequencies" in your preferred music app, like Apple Music, by searching for the number itself, such as "528 Hz."

   396 Hz – Releases Fear

   417 Hz – Eases and Initiates Change

   528 Hz – Heals and repairs DNA

   639 Hz – Heals Relationships

   741 Hz – Finds Creative Expression and Solutions

   852 Hz – Induces Spiritual Homecoming

2. Greet yourself when you wake. Feel your heartbeat and invite in your guides and guardian angel for the day. I use a line from author James Van Praagh: "I am happy, healthy, and holy." I repeat this several times (and I let my kids hear me say it).

3. Invite your guides to go ahead of you, aligning you with people and circumstances for your highest and best good.

4. Connect to your earthly source. Feel the crisp air coming in a cracked window, look to see if the moon is visible at night, and find a sunny spot to sit during the day.

5. Take a hot bath with Epsom salt and ask the salt to detox from your physical body anything that doesn't belong to you. Watch it all go down the drain.

6. Light candles. Fire is a magical, cleansing element and brings calm and focus. Try lighting one candle in a dark room and spend a few minutes staring into its flame. Make the intention to take on the elements of the flame like intense light, warmth, and strength. (Children should be supervised with fire yet respond well to it as a tool used together.)

7. Burn incense. Incense has been used for thousands of years and provokes memories in us from previous human experiences and faraway places.

8. Use essential oils. Essential oils allow us to have different Earth elements at our fingertips like an arsenal of healing and comfort. Diffuse them or use in a carrier oil on the skin. Not all brands are created equal. I use doTERRA with my family and clients. You can become a wholesale customer, or join my team and become a wellness advocate at my.doterra.com/katmulvaney. Signing up with a starter kit is the best place to begin. Not all essential oils are safe for kids. The book *Gentle Babies: Essential Oils and Natural Remedies for Pregnancy, Childbirth, Infants and Young Children* by Debra Raybern is an excellent resource.

9. Learn to play crystal or Tibetan singing bowls. The sounds from these bowls are excellent at clearing energy and are easy and fun to play. Smaller, handheld bowls are great for bedtime with kids. YouTube has many videos of these bowls' music and Apple music, etc. carries it as well, so you can see how your family responds to the sounds. Also search for sound healing ceremonies in your area; they will blow your mind!

    ▪ Crystal Bowl Resources: Sarah Beebe, Yogasarahbb@gmail.com; and Amanda Domnitz, amanda@soulofyoga.com and www.sacredsoundofthesoul.com

10. Move your body. Exercise and movement of any kind clears energy, which is why people get hooked on running or the gym. Start small and involve your kids.

11. Pay attention to the moon cycles. Our bodies are mostly water, so like the tides of the ocean, our bodies and emotions are affected depending on what phase the moon is in. A new moon, for example, is a time for an intense reboot – a time to fill yourself up, recharge, and dump any lower energies into the trash. A full moon brings heightened tension as we fight to find balance between two extremes, so it's important not to get overly emotional or attached to anything during this phase. Many children will respond well to full moon rituals as simple as walking barefoot at sunset or placing crystals outdoors to be recharged by the full moon.

Chapter 9:

BURN YOUR OBSTACLES

Sometimes I look back to before I woke up to my light and my purpose, and while I was asleep and in pain, I had less responsibility. It was easier to be asleep. It was easier to think I'm alone in this and that what I spend my time doing makes no difference to anyone but myself. But then I learned that I am connected to every single living being, through Source, which has nothing to do with religion or any category humans create like gender or race or wealth. I could sleep no more. I found out there was a party happening while I was asleep, millions of woo woos had been living in joy and freedom and fulfillment because their version of truth and their story of Source was untouched by fear or discrimination. We were all light, and it was the best news of my life.

If you take nothing else from this book, please turn to this one bit of truth when you are struggling: You are light, and you are here for a very special reason to evolve and learn with the souls you've spent eternity loving and challenging. It is a gift to be in these bodies, breathing oxygen, being triggered to heal and given the opportunity to experience Earth with all our physical and spiritual gifts simultaneously. No situation is too far gone to reverse, and the human body can heal itself from anything if given the chance to connect to its source, the earth. And while it's a challenge to change the way we view life, as it's annoying to be woken from a deep sleep, we can find comfort in knowing we are never alone. It's impossible to be alone. I'd rather spend five minutes with the energy of an archangel than hours among sleeping humans I can see and touch.

The spiritual path is a shift in thinking, and you can't undiscover its existence. It's like living in a small town in Iowa your whole life and visiting New York City or Miami. It's quiet and safe in Iowa, but you can never get the lights of NYC or the sunny beaches of Miami out of your head. Suddenly your dreams are exploding in your mind and you know Iowa will never be enough again. From the moment I walked into my spiritual yoga teacher training, I knew I'd never be the same. And every tool they gave me, every truth they awoke in me, I knew it was to pass on to struggling kids. It would be easier to watch Netflix, safer to play it small, and more accepted to pretend I go along with the pile of lies we are teaching parents who are teaching their kids. It would be easier to use medication, stay home, make excuses, avoid life, and cry alone in your room for the child and family situation you thought you'd have. But we can do hard things in order to topple broken systems and set our children up for joy and freedom and fulfillment like we have never dreamed. That is what our children will receive when we stop giving them someone else's opinion about who they should be or what they should do. The message going forward should be: be yourself, whatever that looks like. Shine your light, and stay in touch with your reason for being here.

Listen to Your Gut

None of the doctors and most of the specialists will not want to hear that you've decided to delay, decrease, or stop medication. But they are operating from their human and their ego (EGO= edging God out), and since they aren't thinking about Source at all, they are in fear. Fear is uncomfortable and lonely and a place you don't live anymore. Before you interact with a doctor, step into trust. Surround yourself with the energy of Source, knowing you have a large team of support working hard in your favor. Find peace knowing you're now working with the energy that formed your child's cells, the earth, and that any healing available will come from there, not from mixing chemicals and tricking the body into disguising its symptoms.

Family objections can be challenging and hurtful when we've chosen to walk the more spiritual path of trust in self and Source. Remember that most people have a hard time believing anything they can't see and touch. Also, you know your child more than anyone else. You are the expert on your child, and all doctors you hire are working for you, not the other way around. Stand strong in your decision to walk the path less taken and focus on the progress this way of living has brought your child. The truth about your child is that he or she is accessing more of their brain than your stuck and sleeping family member who is objecting. Remember every soul on Earth, no matter their physical age, is at a different level of spiritual growth or evolution. If the most spiritually aware person is in college, for example, your asleep uncle who is too smart to believe in God may only be operating at a grade four. This is not negative, and your uncle is still lovable and kind. Just like a fourth grader, your uncle cannot make himself learn more or learn as fast as a college student, and there is no point in trying.

***

My Gift to You

To receive an audio recording of the fishbowl exercise with Kat, send an email to hello@katmulvaney.com and let us know you're ready for your "little bit of woo."

Chapter 10

THE NEW YOU

*"Speak to your children as if they are
the wisest, kindest, most beautiful and
magical humans on earth, for what they believe
is what they will become."*
– Brooke Hampton

G oing forward, think of yourself as a flame-keeper or flame-tender. Between conception and age seven, our children need their light to be protected. If your child is over the age of seven, we are working to reignite their light–to bring them back from the expectations of others and back into the wisdom of their hearts. Children can feel our desires or demands of them. We project our own fears and failed dreams on them without intending to, and along the way they lose touch with why they're here. Where do they stop and their parent begins? "Mom doesn't talk about X subject, so it must be off-limits or not real." Tell them you're learning more about our Source, or God. Ask them questions about what they remember from before they were born. They know and recall a lot and will surprise and touch you with their words.

Ask them what their body and heart tell them. Release all expectations and get to know your child's authentic self. Ask yourself more questions when facing resistance like "why am I saying no, truly?" and become the witness more often when engaging with your kids. Topple the remains of the broken belief systems that stood so long in your mind–the ones constructed by your ancestors and passed on to you by your parents. Remember your intention to break the cycle of unconsciousness. Trust your children came with all the knowledge they need to settle into their reason for living, which can lead to nothing but joy. Be yourself in front of them and seek out experiences that make your soul sing. Your child is watching you to learn how to thrive through happiness and connection. Happiness is a choice and is available to everyone all the time. It won't fall in our laps or just happen because we graduate with honors or get that sports scholarship. It comes from learning we have all the answers inside of us, and if we follow our inner guidance–our intuition, our gut, our truth, our "GPS"–we will easily and happily know what we want and feel confident and comfortable to ask for the support to get there.

Protecting Your Child, Healing Yourself

Trauma before age eight will become part of children's fabric, so let them play to learn and relax without worrying about the outer world's expectations. When they're small, protect them from negative people and other children who are being taught to be unconscious. Nothing is as important as happiness and peace. Straight As or achievement alone will not lead to happiness. Only emotional health and connection can get you there. Parents must pause and consider what more they needed themselves as children. Consider your toughest character flaws and make a guess as to what in your childhood reinforced this trait. Someone taught you that behavior works. How can you heal it now in a way that will benefit your child and your future grandchildren? That power is within you. Your wounds are not your fault, but your healing is your responsibility alone.

Whatever kids want to learn is the right answer. Whatever activities excite them–hip hop dancing or hula hooping–is the right choice. Let go of everything you were taught about what kids should do and be and trust the soul in front of you who has insight and connection you cannot fathom. Let them help you remember your own. Ask if they remember why they chose to be born at this time, or ask what their special purpose is. Give them confidence by telling them they know their body. Practice using eye contact with them and tell them the eyes are the windows into the soul. Plant seeds with them, and welcome their curiosity. Invite them to participate in family decisions because you honor their opinion, and find appropriate times to tell them things that foster security, confidence, and trust. Here are a few examples to practice:

"I trust you."

"I'm so happy to be your parent."

"Thank you for choosing me to be your parent."

"I love the way you take care of your body."

"You know your body. What is it telling you today?"

"How is your heart today?"

"Is there anything you want to talk about?"

"How can I help?"

"I am always here for you, and nothing you do can make me love you more or less."

And just as importantly, we work to reignite the light in you, the parent. Many of the children this book discusses have come to save us, believe it or not, and now you're in on the plan. You can willingly participate in your own healing as you save your child from the pain I experienced. If saying the statements in the previous paragraph feels unnatural, don't give up. I was not taught this way of parenting or being. I've had to practice. I had to have enough discomfort in life to realize what I experienced as a child was traumatizing and was the cause of my disconnection, pain, and darkness later in life. I decided to focus my work on helping parents find connection with their kids and saving them from years of confusion and quite possibly death. I had to meditate a lot on my inner child. What did I need as a child that I did not receive? How can I give it to my kids from day one and then teach others to do the same? I found out the answers, and my healing doubled the day I decided I was going to parent for connection. I would not pass on the patterns of my parents.

What Success Looks Like

Let me introduce you to Henry. Henry is seven now, but when he was a little younger, he had to stop going to school because it made him angry all the time and he ended up covering his ears most of the day or sitting by himself. His parents divorced because of his behavior and their inability to find him any relief. When things seemed to be getting worse, his mother's friend recommended that she work with me. We met via Skype three days later, and within a week, Henry learned from his mom that he lived inside a fishbowl. He also learned about the feelings each color has and how he can use them to feel better and fix things when he feels upset. His mother and I worked together for six weeks at first, and now Henry says he loves school because his super-powers make him strong and even invisible. His family incorporated a nighttime routine of visualization and talking to Source, and Henry is sleeping better than he has in his life with no more night terrors or talk of monsters coming in the windows.

***

Molly is fifteen, and her parents reached out to me after trying every option they could find to help her with her emotions. When we began working together, Molly hadn't been at school more than three times a week since high school began a few months earlier. Typically, something would upset her during her morning routine, and she would be so devastated she'd refuse to leave home, or she'd cry the whole way to school and then refuse to get out of the car. She would study at home, where she said she concentrated better, and she had OK grades, but she was vulnerable and isolated, and her parents had discovered evidence of self-harm that wasn't getting better. She'd also been making disturbing threats about running away or killing herself whenever she was most upset. Her parents were concerned she'd eventually turn to alcohol or drugs, like many of her peers had already done, and they were understandably experiencing turmoil in other parts of their life because of Molly's delicate situation. After her parents worked through my initial program, they said it was like a lightbulb had been turned on. They said they suddenly understood their daughter so much more, and they felt relaxed for the first time in years.

They spoke to her about the things they were learning and the shifts they were making for themselves, and it was no surprise to me that Molly began acting and feeling a lot better before she ever tried my program herself. After the parents' sixth week working with me, I began having Skype calls with Molly herself. She was excited and relieved to hear her hard emotions were not her fault or even her own. She responded well to the fishbowl exercise, and she lights up every time we talk about it. Since visualization clicked with her so well, she now clears and protects herself every morning before school with color and intention. She also has a new morning routine where she chooses a crystal for each pocket and an affirmation for the day to repeat in her head and carry like a love note on a piece of paper. She's even shared her new information with a close friend, and several kids have asked about her rad crystals.

Molly knows now she is powerful and a very important slice of Source. Before, she said she thought believing in God was dumb, even though she kind of felt a connection, because previous explanations didn't make sense. Life makes more sense now for Molly; she is excited to know there is a name for what she experiences, there is nothing wrong with her (only a bunch of right!), and there are even millions of other kids who feel like her.

Her dad emailed to tell me Molly had attended her first full week of school since elementary school. He said it was thanks to the new tools I had taught her. I assured him it was also their open-mindedness and trust in their daughter that had allowed Molly the room to move into herself and learn about concepts that were the solution for more issues than they'd imagined.

***

Drew was found to be on the Autism spectrum when he was almost three. His parents noticed something different and special about him from birth, and while he is precious to them, his behavior is challenging and keeps them home a lot. He's now eleven, and the biggest challenge is getting out the door and getting inside a destination like a grocery store or an activity he typically enjoys like the zoo. Drew is high functioning, meaning he is fairly independent and learns and plays well at home, but when the external energies of unfamiliar people or places come in, he seems to breakdown and retreat more inside of himself. I worked with Drew's parents for six weeks, and at the end of each call, we discussed how to best explain each concept to Drew. His happiness and peace were our biggest goal, and while we know nothing is a cure-all, it is very obvious Drew responds to energy. His mother clears herself in the morning, clears the house, and clears the car (which takes seconds), and she sets an intention for herself. Before Drew even wakes up, his environment is prepared and ready to gently greet him. Then, Drew has a bag of tricks to use during his day, just like the character in the Zelda video game, and he loves this imagery.

***

I am healing as I preserve my babies' light. I am restored as I reach for my coping tools–tools my babies will carry like torches into the world, lighting their way and spreading the light to others, including my future grandchildren and generations to come. By ending the cycles of unconsciousness, we are doing God's work and evolving the human race. And like I discussed in the previous chapter: This is all new to me. Like a person with a brain injury who loses the use of his limbs, I am in unchartered territory, having to move and operate in completely new ways. While I have to be patient, knowing I can and will accomplish this challenge, I take it one day and one step at a time, reaching for and utilizing the tools I know will get my family to where we want to be – connected and at peace.

SUGGESTED READING

The Snowglobe by Marisa and Joseph Moris

Change Your Aura, Change Your Life by Barbara Martin and Dimitri Moraitis

The Conscious Parent and *The Awakened Family* by Dr. Shefali Tsabary

Dying to Be Me by Anita Moorjani

Hold On to Your Kids: Why Parents Need to Matter More Than Peers by Gordon Neufeld and Gabor Maté

Medical Medium: Secrets Behind Chronic and Mystery Illness and How to Finally Heal by Anthony William

Nourishing Traditions: The Cookbook That Challenges Politically Correct Nutrition and the Diet Dictocrats by Sally Fallon and Mary Enig

Gut and Psychology Syndrome: Natural Treatment for Autism, Dyspraxia, A.D.D., Dyslexia, A.D.H.D.,

Depression, Schizophrenia by Natasha Campbell-McBride

The Crystal Bible: A Definitive Guide to Crystals by Judy Hall

Gentle Babies: Essential Oils and Natural Remedies for Pregnancy, Childbirth, Infants and Young Children by Debra Raybern

ACKNOWLEDGMENTS

Thank you to Flossie Park, my first spiritual teacher, for telling me to remember who I am. You changed my life by introducing me to my light, which forever affected how I would mother and serve others. Thank you, Trisha Kelly (Flossie's sister!), for teaching me the power of color and self-healing, and about true peace. Thank you, Marisa Moris, for the snow globe, for teaching me about my personal power, about being on fire, and about being the real and highest me. The direction Source delivered to me through you will save lives and spread light. Thank you, Angela Lauria, for holding space for the creation of a movement. You've taught me the true meaning of "let go, let God." Thank you to the whole team at The Author Incubator—you are doing God's work! Thank you, Laura Lee, for teaching me about God's love before I saw and felt it for myself. Thank you, Leo Ostreicher, for being my first reader and biggest supporter of my written truth. Thank you to the universe, my Source, and my parents for teaching me about contrast so I could spread truth and light. You played your roles and made me who I am. Thank you, VR and TF, for choosing me. Please always remember who you are. Thank you, Brian, for always saying yes. The universe had such big plans with us. I love you.

Thank you to David Hancock and the Morgan James Publishing team for helping me bring this book to print.

THE DAYS AHEAD

Thank you so much for reading *A Good Day at School*. Since you have reached this point in the book, I know you are committed to mastering your emotions, passing this insight on to your child, and living your family's best life. You are ready to take your family from surviving to thriving. You are ready to experience the authentic people you and your child came here to be, without any outside energetic influences. And I'm ecstatic for you.

To support you and your child through this process, email me at hello@katmulvaney.com to set up a complimentary consultation to see if we are a match to work together. In addition, find me on Facebook and tag your progress with #AskMeAboutYourLight and #ALittleBitOfWoo.

Praying for your highest potential and greatest joy,

Kat Mulvaney

Portland, Oregon

March 2019

ABOUT THE AUTHOR

Kat Mulvaney is a holistic parent coach who teaches parents about their struggling child's emotions and how to move from surviving to thriving. She is leading a movement teaching kids about the power they hold over emotion and energy and to reduce substance abuse and suicide in young people. Kat is a Reiki Master, clairvoyant, and empath and specializes in helping similarly gifted children – along with their parents – who do not conform to many of today's broken systems. She holds a BA in English and communications from Oglethorpe University and has worked to teach people about their power and divinity since 2014, helping families connect to their deepest purpose as individuals and a collective, bringing light and truth to the earth at a time of great evolution and potential. Kat has completed over three hundred hours of spiritual yoga teacher training, holds a fifty-hour children's yoga certification, and a metaphysician certificate from the Spiritual Arts Institute in San Diego, California. She resides in Portland, Oregon, with her husband, two children, and Jack Russell terrier and enjoys nature, CrossFit, locally grown food, sound healing, listening to the universe, and hot baths. Her website is www.katmulvaney.com.